Laura Andreini

essays by

Sara Benzi
Matteo Moscatelli
Jörn Walter

ON THE ROAD city
Hamburg

ON THE ROAD
Editor of collection
Laura Andreini

editorial project
Forma Edizioni srl, Firenze, Italia
redazione@formaedizioni.it
www.formaedizioni.it

editorial direction
Laura Andreini

authors
Laura Andreini

editorial staff
Sara Benzi
Maria Giulia Caliri
Livia D'Aliasi
Valentina Muscedra

graphic design
Silvia Agozzino
Isabella Peruzzi

translations
Miriam Hurley
Katy Hannan

texts by
Laura Andreini
Sara Benzi
Roberto Bosi
Matteo Moscatelli (pp. 28-29, 38-39, 74-75, 76-77, 92-93, 100-101, 174-175)
Jörn Walter

Second Edition: August 2020

ISBN 978-88-55210-45-4

Table of Contents

Guidebook as a tool

On the Road is a collection of contemporary architecture guidebooks whose purpose is to tell about a place, whether a city or larger area, through its architectural works chosen to be visited and experienced directly.

The guidebook has a convenient special jacket that opens into a map marking the location of the architectural works and interesting sites to visit. On the back are miniature images and addresses of the architectural works described in detail within.

The book starts with short essays explaining the city or area's present day and history and outlining possible future scenarios with planned or imminent projects. Each work features a photograph of the whole, an architectural drawing (plan or section), a short description, and facts including architect, type, year of construction, address, website, and how to visit it.

The finest architecture of each city and suggested routes are represented by this collection of not-to-be-missed, "timeless" buildings that uniquely define their settings. General information and useful tips for travelers help them optimize their visits and quickly understand the essence of the place described.

Museums, theatres, restaurants, hotels and a list of top architectural firms working in the city let visitors turn a regular trip into an opportunity for study or work.

Note: The pinpoints outside the maps at the beginning of the itineraries are viewable on the rear of the book jacket.

Hamburg

Laura Andreini*

Five years after the publication of the Hamburg Guide, the first of the On the Road series, it was decided to print a new updated version to include recently constructed projects of considerable interest which have been integrated into the five itineraries proposed in the guide. When discussing contemporary architecture, constant updating is a fundamental aspect, especially in those cities intent on maintaining their objectives of high urban planning standards. For this reason, even after only a few years, the first edition ran the risk of being out of date.

In 2011 Hamburg was awarded the title of European Green Capital by the European Commission, and almost ten years later, it continues to demonstrate its avant-garde stature in the field of urban development, recovery of decommissioned buildings and brownfield land, development of green urban areas and sustainable mobility.

Hamburg has continued to implement its farsighted program which did not cease after the initial changes, but which advanced, creating a network of buildings and infrastructures that confirm the excellent livability levels of German cities. It represents a case study for contemporary designers, because it shows a strategic opportunity for changing and maintaining certain standards that can be used as examples for many European cities currently involved in the adjustments necessary for the change from heavy industry to the green economy.

The Niederhafen River Promenade, designed by Zaha Hadid Architects, and opened in 2019, confirmed the city's aim of evolving according to the criteria of improving the life of its citizens. This promenade, 625 meters long, does not simply form a connection system, but offers new services and possibilities for easy mobility, while reinforcing the protection wall against river flooding. This was obtained while providing Hamburg with an urban landmark able to stand alongside the architectural prestige of the Elbphilharmonie concert hall designed by Herzog & de Meuron, an emblem that demonstrates how contemporary architecture can be layered within the existing fabric to become a symbol for the city. Although they are featured in two separate itineraries, these projects are only a few hundred meters apart, and bear witness to the desire, now successfully accomplished, to redevelop the area of the old port which was in a state of neglect until a few years ago. Alongside the HafenCity workshops and the IBA "new city", this objective demonstrates how Hamburg was able to reinvent itself beginning with the understanding of its own potential and focusing on new interventions from the viewpoint of sustainable living.

Today Hamburg forms an open-air museum for contemporary architecture lovers and an authentic observatory on the realizations and benefits possible with creative sustainable urban planning.

* Architect and Associate Professor at DIDA, University of Florence. Co-founder of Studio Archea where she still works, she is also writer and deputy editor for *area* magazine.

Political / geographical facts

country
Germany

language
german

area code
0049 (0)40

coordinates
53° 33' 02'' N
9° 59' 36'' E

area
755.22 sq. km

population
1,841,179

density
2,430 inhabitants / sq.km

time zone
UTC+1

city website
www.hamburg.de

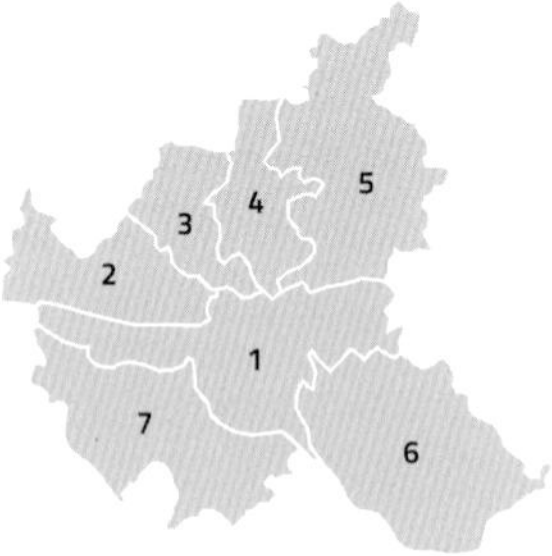

Administrative districts

1. Hamburg-Mitte
2. Altona
3. Eimsbüttel
4. Hamburg-Nord
5. Wandsbek
6. Bergedorf
7. Harburg

General information

useful addresses and numbers

INFORMATION OFFICES

Hamburg Information
Hamburg Central Station
(U/S-Bahn Hauptahnhof)
Kirchenallee Main Entrance
+49 (0)40 30051300
Mon - Sat / 9 am - 9 pm
Sun and public holidays / 10 am - 6 pm
December 24 / 10 am - 4 pm
Jan 1 / 11 am - 6 pm

HafenCity InfoCenter im Kesselhaus
Am Sandtorkai 30, 20457 Hamburg
+49 (0)40 36901799
Tue - Sun / 10 am - 6 pm
Mon / closed
May - September
Thu / 10 am - 8 pm

IBA Dock
Am Zollhafen 12, 20539 Hamburg
+49 (0)40 2262270

EMERGENCY SERVICES

Ambulance and Fire Department 112
Police 110
Emergency medical service +49 (0)40 228022
24-hour Pharmacy +49 (0)40 22833

URBAN TRANSPORTATION*

Bus
bus tickets from the driver
www.hvv.de

U-Bahn (underground network - 4 lines)
tickets: from orange vending machines at the station entrances
www.hvv.de

S-Bahn (urban rail network - 6 lines)
tickets: from orange vending machines at the station entrances
www.hvv.de

Hafenfähren im HVV (river network - 6 lines)
www.hadag.de

Taxi +49 (0)40 441011, +49 (0)40 666666,
Großraumtaxi (up to 8 people) +49 (0)40 80007000

Bicycle rentals

StadtRAD
Automatic rental system at public bike stations in different points throughout the city, which have an electronic device that lets you use a credit card to register for the rental system.
stadtrad.hamburg.de

Hamburg City Cycles
St. Pauli - Bernhard-Nocht-Straße 89-91,
20359 Hamburg
+49 (0)40 74214420
Mon - Sun / 9.30 am - 6.30 pm
www.hhcitycycles.de

Fahrradstation Dammtor | Rotherbaum
Schlüterstraße 11, 20146 Hamburg
+49 (0)40 41468277
Mon - Fri / 10 am - 1 pm, 2 pm - 6 pm

CONSULATE GENERAL OF ITALY

area jurisdiction
Consulate General of Hannover
Mon / 3 pm - 5 pm
Tue, Thu, Fri / 9 am - 12 pm
Wed / 9 am - 12 am / 3 pm - 5 pm
Main phone line +49 (0)40 511283790

BRITISH CONSULATE GENERAL

Neuer Jungfernstieg 20 / Fehland Straße 3
20354 Hamburg
+49 (0)40 44803236
by appointment only

HOW TO DIAL

From a local landline: dial just the number

From a foreign landline: dial international prefix (+49), Hamburg's area code (40) and the number.

From a foreign mobile phone: dial international prefix (+49), a zero (0), Hamburg's area code (40) and the number.

* We recommend the Hamburg Card, which entitles you to unlimited travel on all public transportation systems in Hamburg, free entrance or discounts at many museums, theaters and tourist attractions.

Useful tips

Roberto Bosi*

1. Recommended overnight accommodations according to budget. High: **Empire Riverside Hotel/49**, designed by David Chipperfield. Medium: **Raphael Hotel Wälderhaus/75**, in the middle of the IBA area, a model of sustainability for Hamburg. Low: Superbude, a small chain of hostels with a sophisticated design; two locations: St. Pauli (in the St. Pauli district) and St. Georg (behind the Hamburg Hauptbahnhof).

2. We suggest the Hamburg Card for getting around Hamburg (there are 1-, 3-, or 5-day options). They can be bought individually or for groups of up to 5 people. The Card can also be used for public transportation in Großbereich Hamburg (Greater Hamburg Area, including all parts of the city and its suburbs) and entitles you to discounts on many services, such as short cruises on the harbor and the River Alster, which is an excellent way to see the city from the water.

3. To fully understand the history of Hamburg and the power of the Hanseatic League, be sure to visit the Internationales Maritimes Museum Hamburg, a museum about maritime history and studies.

4. To understand the urban renewal in progress, be sure to visit HafenCity, starting at its information centers: **Kesselhaus/32**, a building linking the historic Speicherstadt district and HafenCity. The Speicherstadt district's former thermal power station is now home to a 1:500 scale of HafenCity, showing the construction stages to date, future plans, and illustrating the diverse economic relationships between HafenCity and the city of Hamburg. Another information center is at Osaka 9, HafenCity Pavilion, which focuses on the district's sustainability.
Interesting guided tours of the districts can be organized upon request in these information centers.

5. We suggest visiting **IBA Hamburg/69**, created during the International Building Exhibition 2013, directed by Uli Hellweg, with over 50 projects aiming to build a new city of the future. The building houses the "IBA at Work" exhibition.

6. To learn about Hamburg's historic architecture, we suggest visiting **Sprinkenhof/19** by Fritz Höger, Hans and Oskar Gerson, 1927-1943.

7. In inclement weather, you can find a nice refuge full of art masterpieces in **Hamburger Kunsthalle/16** with an expansion designed by Oswald Mathias Ungers.

8. While covering the Center-North route, it is well worth a visit to the **Youth Music School/59** by Benedetta Tagliabue – Miralles Tagliabue EMBT. You can tour it by prior arrangement or, with a little luck, you might chance to see it while attending a concert put on there.

9. A must-see is the **Elbphilharmonie/44**, concert hall designed by Herzog & de Meuron as a vertical extension of an old cocoa warehouse. Beyond the new project's architectural interest, it can be an excellent chance for a special night out to attend a concert.

10. The Empire Riverside Bar is on the 20th floor of the hotel (**Empire Riverside Hotel/49**) designed by David Chipperfield. Treating yourself to a nice break here can be the perfect way to top off your evening in style and admire Hamburg from above.

* Architect and Director of ProViaggiArchitettura; contributes to industry periodicals and pursues research at DIDA in Florence.

From Hammaburg to Hamburg: the history of a city built on canals

Sara Benzi*

Inextricably linked to the North Sea, the River Elbe and its tributaries, Hamburg owes these bodies of waters its origins, its growth, and its fortune, as well as its recovery from destruction time and time again and from the difficult periods it gone through over the centuries.

The first traces of a settlement here date back to the Stone Age. However, it was not until the ninth century that there is mention of a site, between the River Alster and the River Elbe, called "Hammaburg" ('Hamma' is of unknown origins; 'burg' is from fortress). A fortress may have protected a Baptistery built at the behest of Charlemagne in 810 to Christianize the region when he extended his reign here.

Its position on the Empire's northern edge was a contributing factor to the city being destroyed and rebuilt nine times until 1139. That was the year that a charter was written by Frederick I, known as Red Beard, which ensured Hamburg ships safe passage on the River Elbe, conferring Hamburg the status of "Free Imperial City". Despite the charter's authenticity being uncertain, the letter, dated May 7, 1189, and still celebrated on Hafengeburstdag was valid until 1888 when Hamburg's customs free zone was formed with duty-free access, which, combined with the vicinity of primarily trade routees of the North Sea and the Baltic Sea made Hamburg northern Europe's largest port. The port is at the junction between ocean navigation and inland navigation, which was strengthened starting in 1241 when it formed a trade alliance with Lubeck. This laid the foundations for the Hanseatic League, a powerful association between northern German and Baltic cities united in cooperative alliances starting in the twelfth century.

When Hamburg was declared a Free Imperial City in 1510, the middle class was strengthened as it was made of craft guilds the reflected Hamburg's new economic horizons. This also fostered a climate of peace, aided by its embracing of Lutheranism in 1529, putting it outside of religious wars. For example, during the seventeenth century, after becoming the site of the first stock exchange (1558) and the first bank (1619), the Thirty Years War (1618-1648) barely affected it. Nonetheless, after major efforts by part of the population to make the city safer by building a city wall, internal social unrest erupted in the seventeenth and eighteenth centuries; that, along with repeated attacks by the Danes, caused economic stagnation, from which it recovered only at the end of the eighteenth century after opening trade with the United States. At the dawn of the nineteenth century, Hamburg was one of Europe's most prosperous ports, but in 1806 it was occupied by the French and annexed to the empire as the capital of the Bouches-de-l'Elbe department. Russian forces liberated it with the Congress of Vienna in 1814-1815 and it was again a sovereign state. Trade resumed, particularly transoceanic trade and with Britain, laying the foundations for Hamburg's prosperity, bolstered by the dawn of the industrial era. Hamburg became home of the empire's greatest shipyards, a booming population and the site of major urban expansions and transformation.

In 1842 about a third of Hamburg was destroyed by what would be remembered as the "Great Fire". Reconstruction took more than 40 years and led to building great Baroque city walls, covering two canals and construction of new houses in a classicist style. Also of great significance was the building of the warehouse area, starting in 1881, distinguished by the exclusive use of red bricks. The closed port, exempt from customs duties, helped turn Hamburg into one of the world's largest warehouse and trade centers.

During World War I, the forced interruption of maritime activities caused another period of crisis. At the end of the war, Germany lost its colonies, which meant Hamburg lost its trade routees. At the top of priorities was building social housing and a new ring of residential districts arose around the city center with the architect Fritz Schumacher leading the way. This urban renewal was, however, undermined by the devastating air raids of World War II. Hamburg was reduced to 43 million cubic meters of rubble, making its fate comparable to that of Dresden. Post-war reconstruction, whose emblem was the building of 12 skyscrapers between 1946 and 1956 in the Herverstehude district, was slow and hampered by the 1962 flood that damaged much of the city center.

After German reunification in 1990, Hamburg began to strive to regain its dominance as a leading commercial port and a city at the forefront socially and in urban planning. These were the foundations for the urban planning and economic "miracle" currently underway, giving impetus to major urban projects like HafenCity and IBA.

* Architect and PhD in architectural history, active in teaching and publishing.

Sustainable experiments in redeveloping the port city

Matteo Moscatelli*

Hamburg is the second largest port city in Europe and one of the ten largest by population. It is undergoing a period of great change brought both by specific redevelopment projects of some strategic areas and a new design approach striving for widespread quality of life. In 2011 Hamburg was recognized as a Green Capital. The city has set meaningful sustainability goals for itself, focusing on reducing CO_2 emissions by 80% by 2050) with development policies implemented on many levels. In terms of energy savings, Hamburg benefits from a well-organized district heating network, whose coal-based power is soon to be integrated with co-generation systems from geothermal and solar sources and from heat recovery from the waste of industrial processes.

Its mobility plan incentivizes acting with greater respect for environment. This entails public transportation being organized so no city dwellers live more than 300 from a stop; foot traffic has increased thanks to more efficient traffic management, as has bike traffic with 1,700 kilometers of reserved cycle lanes.

Population growth forecast for the next few years will be matched by more responsible land protection policies, focused on redeveloping brownfield sites rather than taking over new spaces. A recent example is in the Falkenried neighborhood in a 50,000 square meter area in the residential part of Eppendorf. Choices such as restoring several existing buildings (city transport vehicles were manufactured here and using traditional local building materials (such as Wittmund brick), the design by BOLLES+WILSON (2004-2005) proved it an example of sustainability extended to the cultural sphere as well.

We can also consider the example of IBA (2013). Its objectives (as seen in works like the Algenhaus, the **Energy Bunker**, and International Garden Show) go beyond the short-term goal for exhibitions to include later conversion into an urban development for zero consumption living.

The most important project in recent years is one of the largest in size in contemporary European architecture, the HafenCity project, located on a 155-hectare area between the historic city center and the Elbe River. Once completed, it will increase the city's size by 40%. The plan's gestation period started in the eighties with a number of studies (approved by the regional parliament in 1999). The project entails 12,000 new homes for 40,000 inhabitants, and 40,000 jobs. The series of studies laid the foundation for the 1999 competition won by the ASTOC-Kees Christiaanse-Hamburgplan group, with further fine-tuning later. HafenCity is organized in 13 different districts, each in a different state of progress (some areas are already inhabited; others are under construction, while others are still in the design phase), and each with a different intended use (services, homes, businesses, and recreation). Another model project for this part of the city and beyond is Herzog & de Meuron's **Elbphilharmonie**. The building contains a 2,150 seat concert hall, a hotel, cafes, restaurants, and an elevated square. It is a former brick warehouse on which a new structure is set, made of glass panels, bent and cut to foster natural ventilation.

The new residential and office buildings served as a testing grounds for state-of-the-art building techniques and building system components: the **Baufeld 10** building (2007-2008) by LOVE architecture and urbanism, has highly efficient foam polyurethane insulation and a system of adjustable solar collectors that accumulate excess thermal energy. For **Unilever Headquarters** (2007-2009) by Behnisch Architekten a cooling system was designed with thermally activated concrete slabs; an external coating on the glazed facade protects from the elements, and a SMD-LED lighting system is used, which is 70% more efficient than traditional halogen lights. Attention to ecological issues is extended to other areas as well, such as mobility, with a more efficiently organized network of pedestrian and cycling paths than in other parts of the city, and emission reduction, 27% less than neighborhoods powered by natural gas.

The examples of IBA and HafenCity demonstrate how the city of Hamburg's interest is not simply focused on energy-saving objectives but also in the ways in which the issue of sustainability is understood. As these recent projects show, sustainability pertains to more than the architectural scale to include the urban scale as well, and sustainability does not mean only environmental sustainability; it also means economic, social and cultural sustainability.

* Architect and PhD, teaches at the Politecnico University in Milan and at IED Design Milano.

Architectural Culture in Hamburg

Jörn Walter*

Hamburg's urban redevelopment over the last twenty years has been highly dynamic and entailed a fresh model that reconsidered development potentials within the existing city and its orientation towards the Elbe River. The rediscovery of the city on the water and its amphibious nature, through projects such as 'string of pearls' (Perlenkette), 'Hafencampus Harburg', 'HafenCity' and 'Leap across the Elbe' (Sprung über die Elbe), were major drivers for pushing urban and architectural planning towards new achievements. They were not only aesthetic considerations, as they also entailed ecological, social, and economic renewal. It has been said that Hamburg is reinventing itself. Perhaps, but the examples written about here show how Hamburg has stayed truer to its nature than it might seem at first glance. Despite the renewal needed, the city's traditional broad outlines are still a major frame of reference. Ideas for the future are found by keeping well in mind its origins.

When we look for Hamburg's architectural features, we immediately come to brick and white plaster, which have always marked the city's external image and continue to do so, though joined by other materials, primarily wood and sandstone, followed by cement, glass, and finally metal and plastic surfaces. If we study more in depth, we see that its distinctive traits are in shunning an overly exuberant representation of itself, favoring instead tasteful subtlety and reserved elegance. This is surely linked to Hamburg being one of the oldest republican cities in which a single ruler has never been able to determine historical events. Another major factor is that Hamburg's present-day image goes back to the influences of twentieth-century classicism and influences of the 1920s and post-war Modernism, in many ways, both in terms of quantity and quality. Ultimately, it must have been the spirit of the Enlightenment that suited the city's spirit and made its deep mark on its architecture, the pursuit of order in accord with reason, nature, democratic and liberal, humane, and harmonious.

In this Enlightenment spirit, Hamburg's architecture has pursued a Modernist project; however, this is no longer the revolutionary, utopian-social architecture of the 1920s, nor the complacent, acritical Modernism of the post-war era. It seeks to be rooted neither in the past nor in newness. This Modernism is self-critical, sometimes doubting, sometimes fresh, and sometimes just different. It seeks to recalibrate the best aesthetics of the twentieth century on the basis of changing economic, ecological, and social demands. This architecture is rooted to the ground with low-environmental impact and high social utility. This approach to urban architecture is less monotonous, considerably more diverse and more emotive, and there is, of course, a re-exploration of materials and forms too.

This emerges from HafenCity's buildings, which seek a relationship with the scale of Hamburg's city center. With a high degree of mixed functions there is also an intentional diversity of images, variety, and urban vitality instead of the monotonous quality of large twentieth-century expansions. It is seen in the architecture for the Internationale Bauausstellung (IBA - International Building Exhibition) on Elbe's islands. To an extraordinary degree, they have committed themselves to ecological and social renewal at affordable prices, as well as overcoming fragmentation of the city fabric on the outlying areas through high quality connecting spaces. It is seen in Hamburg's new icon, the **Elbphilharmonie** which (through a curved roof and glass facade, as extraordinary in its technology as it is in its aesthetics) on the preserved outside walls of an old warehouse on the pier. This is a new, exciting approach to the city and its culture, known heretofore only by connoisseurs.

All these projects are focused on forming new identities. Their aim is not to go against that which is familiar, but to complement and enrich it. This architecture guide's selection of large and small architectural projects, both contemporary and historic, invites us to learn about the amphibious, green city that is Hamburg and its path to a sustainable, twenty-first-century metropolis. We hope it also inspires readers to come in person to visit and delve into our city.

* Architectural Director, Planning and Environment Department of the City of Hamburg.

Mahnmahl St. Nikolai
Hamburger Rathaus
Alsterfleet
Niederhafen River Promenade

C - Deichtor
fice Center
Spiegel Group Offices
Cinnamon Tower
Coffee Plaza
Kibbelstegbrücke
HafenCity Public Space
Elbphilharmonie
Kesselhaus
H2O
© saiko3p / Adobe Stock

Tanzende Türme
Michaeliskirche
Mahnmahl St. Nikolai
Hamburger Rathaus
DOC - Deichtor Office Center
Spiegel Group Offices

Finanzbehörde
Sprinkenhof

Strategies for visiting Hamburg

To tour Hamburg thoroughly, you need five to six days. The guidebook is organized in five routes, each of which takes a full day. At least two days are suggested for the City-Center because of the many buildings that can be toured inside.

Route A | City-Center
The urban fabric in the City-Center is dense and includes Hamburg's old medieval center. The area has many historic buildings, including **Michaeliskirche/01** and **Hamburger Rathaus/09**, as well as contemporary architecture mainly used for residential and service sector uses. Many of its brick buildings, like the historic **Chilehaus/18** and **Finanzbehörde/07** offices, are excellent examples of early twentieth-century Expressionist architecture, well worth a visit, as is the **Hamburger Kunsthalle/16** art museum, designed by Oswald Mathias Ungers.

Route B | HafenCity
The port area south of the City-Center had been in poor condition for many years and is now being developed with a special sustainable experimental project for converting warehouses into residential buildings with adjacent services. The area has an information center set in a former thermal power plant (**Kesselhaus/32**) in Hamburg. Particularly impressive is the spectacular **Elbphilharmonie/44** by Swiss architects Herzog & de Meuron.

Route C | St. Pauli/Altona
West of the City-Center, there is an area called Norderelbe that stretches lengthwise on a branch of the River Elbe. The area is less dense, which lets it be easily visited on foot. We suggest visiting the **Flakturm IV/46**, a concrete bunker from 1942, and the fish market of Altona, the **Fischauktionshalle/51**, which has become one of the city's most charming areas.

Route D | Center-North
The Center-North has more natural features and covers a greater area than the previous routes, which means public transportation is needed to visit it. There are two noteworthy buildings here designed by architect Fritz Schumacher: **Planetarium/64** from 1912-1917 and the **Hamburger Krematorium/65** from 1928-1932.

Route E | IBA
The International Building Exhibition area is a testing ground for more than seventy designs made with the most innovative, eco-sustainable, autonomous energy-producing systems. There is a very complete information office (**IBA Dock/69**) here. Of particular note is the restoration of the Wilhelmsburg (**Energy Bunker/71**), turned into Europe's largest solar power plant.

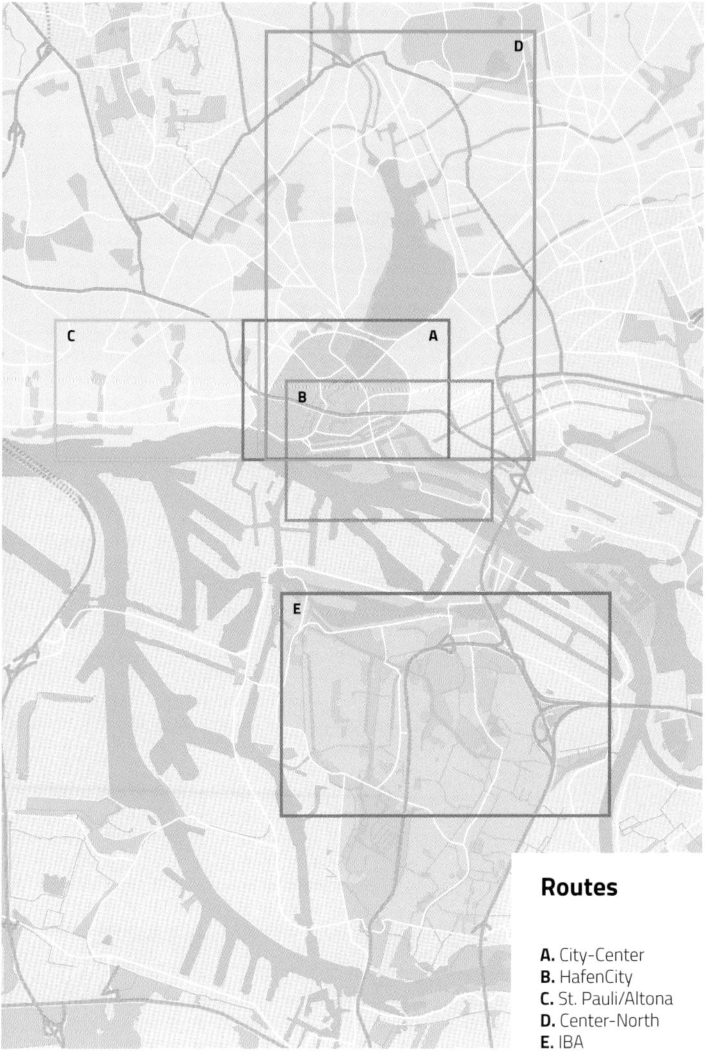

Routes

A. City-Center
B. HafenCity
C. St. Pauli/Altona
D. Center-North
E. IBA

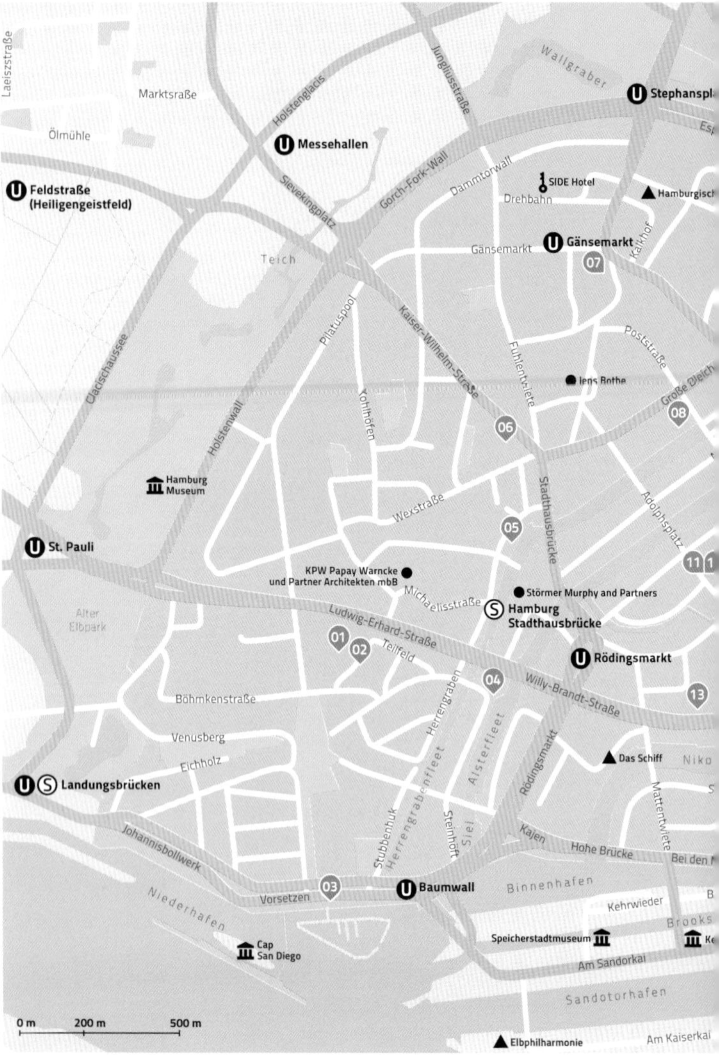
Laeiszstraße
Marktsraße
Ölmühle
Wallgraben
Jungiusstraße
Stephanspl
Messehallen
Holstenglacis
Feldstraße (Heiligengeistfeld)
Sievekingplatz
Gorch-Fock-Wall
Dammtorwall
SIDE Hotel
Drehbahn
Hamburgisch
Gänsemarkt
Gänsemarkt
Kalkhof
07
Teich
Pilatuspool
Kaiser-Wilhelm-Straße
Poststraße
Fuhlentwiete
Jens Bothe
Große Bleich
08
Glacischaussee
Holstenwall
Kohlhöfen
06
Hamburg Museum
Stadthausbrücke
Adolphsplatz
Wexstraße
05
St. Pauli
11
KPW Papay Warncke und Partner Architekten mbB
Michaelisstraße
Störmer Murphy and Partners
Hamburg Stadthausbrücke
Ludwig-Erhard-Straße
Alter Elbpark
01
02
Teilfeld
Rödingsmarkt
Herrengraben
04
Willy-Brandt-Straße
13
Böhmkenstraße
Alsterfleet
Venusberg
Herrengrabenfleet
Rödingsmarkt
Das Schiff
Eichholz
Landungsbrücken
Mattentwiete
Johannisbollwerk
Stubbenhuk
Steinhöft
Siel
Kajen
Hohe Brücke
Bei den
Baumwall
03
Binnenhafen
Niederhafen
Vorsetzen
Kehrwieder
Brooks
Speicherstadtmuseum
Cap San Diego
Am Sandorkai
Sandtorhafen
0 m
200 m
500 m
Elbphilharmonie
Am Kaiserkai

City-Center

01. Michaeliskirche
02. Krayenkamp
03. Niederhafen River Promenade
04. Alsterfleet
05. Deutsch-Japanisches Zentrum
06. Hanse Forum
07. Finanzbehörde
08. Große Bleichen 19
09. Hamburger Rathaus
10. Handelskammer Hamburg
11. Haus im Haus
12. JohannisContor
13. Mahnmal St. Nikolai
14. Steckelhörn 11
15. Domplatz
16. Hamburger Kunsthalle
17. Commercial and Office Building on Lilienstraße
18. Chilehaus
19. Sprinkenhof
20. DOC - Deichtor Office Center

01. Michaeliskirche

Englische Planke 1
20459 Hamburg

May - September
Mon - Sun / 9 am - 7.30 pm
October - April
Mon - Sun / 9 am - 6.30 pm
November - March
Mon - Sun / 10 am - 5.30 pm

+49 (0)40 376780
www.st-michaelis.de

U3
Rödingsmarkt;
Baumwall

S1/S3
Stadthausbrücke

17/37
Michaeliskirche

St. Michael's 132-meter bell tower makes it a landmark in the city. It is one of northern Germany's most beautiful baroque churches after three reconstructions throughout the centuries starting in the mid-seventeenth century: the original church was built between 1647 and 1661 in baroque style and was destroyed by lightning. The second edifice was built between 1750 and 1762 in the shape of a Greek cross and had a copper-clad tall wooden tower added between 1777 and 1786 which was destroyed by fire in 1906. Between 1907 and 1912, the new church was built, which was then bombed in World War II and extensively remodeled between 1983 and 2009.

The church is 52-meter long, 44-meter wide and 27-meter tall. It can accommodate up to 2,500 people in a large area featuring white with golden finishes within which are three unusually important organs.

Eye-catching copper clads the roof and tower supporting Germany's largest clock, with an 8-meter diameter. From the top of the tower visitors enjoy a breathtaking, sweeping view of the Hamburg encompassing its full breadth.

architects	type	construction
-	church	1907-1912

02. Krayenkamp

Krayenkamp 10-11
20459 Hamburg

open to public

Not far from the St. Michael church, past 10 Kayenkamp Street, there is a small courtyard holding a cluster of homes built in the seventeenth century for social purposes, now home to a museum, art gallery, and restaurants. They are known as 'Krameramtsstuben' or 'Krameramtswohnungen' (literally: "office apartments/merchant association").

Built by a merchant association as homes for widows of Hamburg's merchants (in spice, silk, hardware, and so forth) who had to leave their homes attached to the shops. Now they are the oldest buildings in the city center. They were built with the typical wood lattice and brick structure with areas less than 3 meters in width.

The Museum Krameramtsstuben shows visitors an original apartment furnished with mid-nineteenth century furniture.

U3
Rödingsmarkt

S1/S2/S3
Stadthausbrücke;
Landungsbrücken

17/37/641
601/609/610
Michaeliskirche

© Alf Hermann

architects
-

type
residential, commercial, museum

construction
1620-1700

03. Niederhafen River Promenade

Elbpromenade
20459 Hamburg

open to public

U3
Baumwall
(Elbphilharmonie)

111/608
U Baumwall

72
Elbphilharmonie

Located at the meeting point between the city and the water, the River Promenade project replaces one of the city's flood barriers between St. Pauli Landungsbrücken and the Baumwall stop at Niederhafen. The 625 meter walkway has reinforced the river flood prevention system, while providing a prominent new urban landmark at the same time.

The Promenade has a minimum width of 10 meters, and provides a new public space for pedestrians, street artists, and sports enthusiasts. It incorporates restaurants, street level shops and kiosks with public services and tourist info.

The Promenade follows a sinuous route that is not always parallel with the flood barriers; a series of amphitheater-like stairways have been carved out of these curved gaps and face towards the river or the city: their wide steps provide access down to the river and city street levels. The amphitheater stairways are positioned at the points where adjacent neighborhood streets lead towards the riverside area and offer seating space with new views over the river port and marina. Built in contrasting materials they have a strong visual impact.

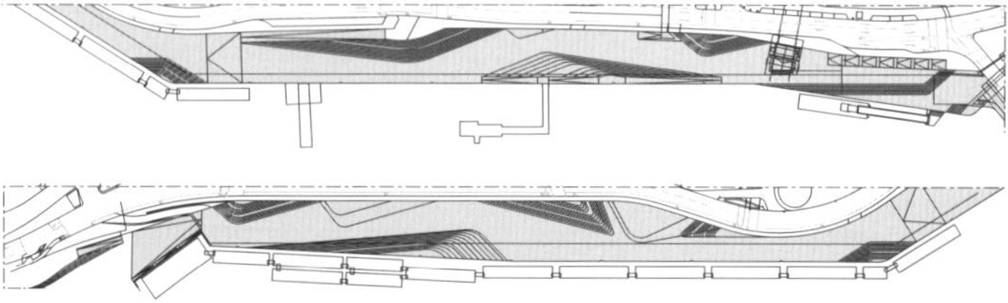

architects
Zaha Hadid Architects

type
public space

construction
2006-2019

04. Alsterfleet

Admiralitätstraße 10 and 14
20459 Hamburg

external view only

U3
Rödingsmarkt

3/31/601/609/610
17/607/608
U Rödingsmarkt
(Großer Burstah)

The Asterfleet project is on the historic Alster canal between the old city to the east and Hamburg's new expansion. The complex consists of an office unit and residential buildings. It is a succession of ten rectangular structures oriented east-to-west and closed by a pentagonal structure made entirely of glass and metal. The buildings are raised one level above the docks on tall pillars that leave a pedestrian passageway underneath that makes for a scenic walkway.

The head building is accessed through a large atrium clad with a double glass envelope that regulates its interior microclimate and interacts with natural light. The building fits into its surroundings through a translucent facade in which a green film is set that creates its color effects, which shift according to the light and reflections off the water. Its bond with the environment is underscored in the apartments, clad with bricks, displaying large glazed walls outstretched towards the river.

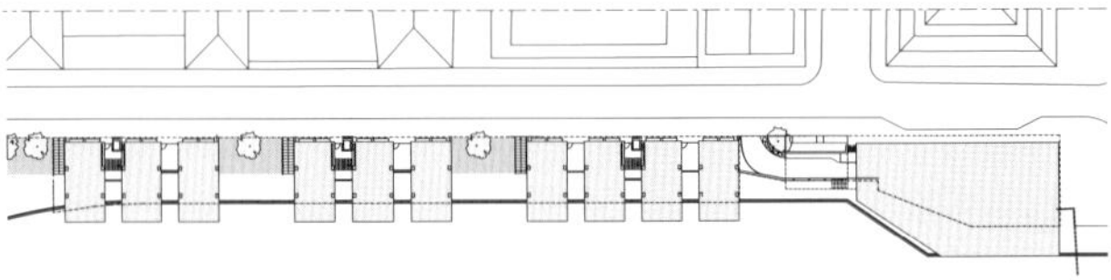

architects
Studio Fuksas

type
offices, residential

construction
1997-2002

05. Deutsch-Japanisches Zentrum

Düsternstraße 1
20355 Hamburg

external view only

U3
Rödingsmarkt

S1/S2/S3
Stadthausbrücke

3/34/607/X35
Axel Springer Square

The German-Japanese Center is made up of two buildings, one of which conceptually represents Japan and the other, Germany. The first building is thin, stretching lengthwise to form a curve along the canal, as if bowing towards the city grid. Both its slender lines and bowing refer to Japanese culture. The second building is a solidly-grounded, clean-lined block, representing the virtues of German culture. On the back of the second building there are tiers on semi-open courtyards, a pedestrian arcade along the Stadthausbrücke forms a section of city space protected from the elements. The facades express strong duality. The street fronts are clad with dark clinker bricks in marked contrast to the glass on the back part. The interiors are organized in terms of function by joining German and Japanese elements such as the combination of a typical office cubicle with an open plan work space.

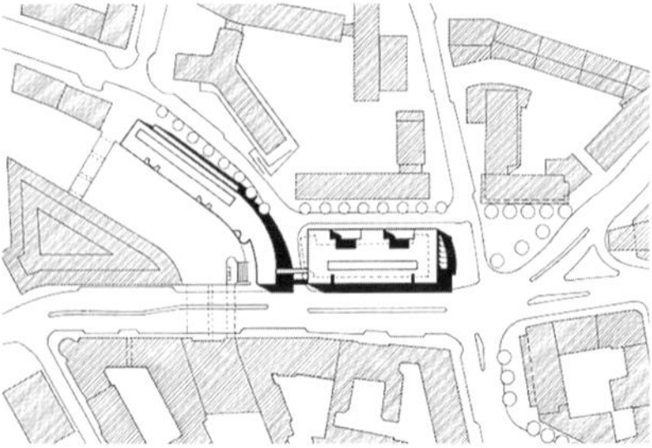

architects
gmp Architekten von Gerkan, Marg und Partner

type
offices

construction
1993-1995

06. Hanse Forum

Axel-Springer-Platz 3
20355 Hamburg

external view only

U2
Gänsemarkt
U3
Rödingsmarkt

S1/S2/S3
Stadthausbrücke

3/34/607/X35
Axel Springer Square

The design creates a covered square at the intersection of two roads as a fluid space connecting two seven-floor office buildings with dramatically-contrasting forms and designs. The two units, one with glazed ceramic balustrades and the other fully glazed, are joined by a single system in terms of form and function. The atrium becomes the cornerstone of the new complex, connecting the two buildings through a series of bridges and stairs.

The atrium has a transparent, heat-insulating glazed exterior designed to provide sound insulation from the heavy traffic of the main road it faces. The building's double glazing minimizes energy loss and is open to ventilation, bolstered by a slat system above and below the floor slabs.

The combination of elements protecting against the Sun (sunbreakers placed between the facade's two panes), for heat insulation and natural air exchange, makes operating the building inexpensive in terms of energy use.

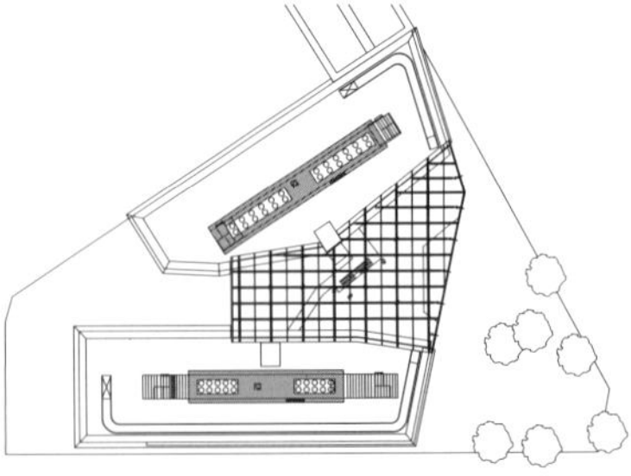

architects
Studio Fuksas

type
offices

construction
1998-2002

07. Finanzbehörde

Gänsemarkt 36
20354 Hamburg

external view only

U2
Gänsemarkt

4/5/19/36/603/ 604/605 602/688
U Gänsemarkt

The Finanzbehörde is considered one of the architect Fritz Schumacher's most important works. He was the Superintendent of Building in Hamburg between 1923 and 1933 and was a major force for innovating the Hanseatic city's face. The grand building rises nine floors high on a rectangular plan. The two main facades converge at a curved corner, which the architect gave particular importance, conceiving it as the primary hinge point for the entire complex.

Despite the grandness of the building, it does not appear too hulking because of its brick cladding, which evokes Hamburg's architectural tradition. It is made dynamic by surfaces of balustrades, pilasters and tiers on the top floors. The design's primary materials are brick and glass, with an exterior design of a quick succession of windows. Brick pilasters suggest the reinforced concrete columns behind them. The entire structural system is made of reinforced concrete. Brick has an exclusively decorative function in cladding the entire building surface. The interior waiting room, in a joint project with Villeroy & Boch, was entirely clad in majolica tiles.

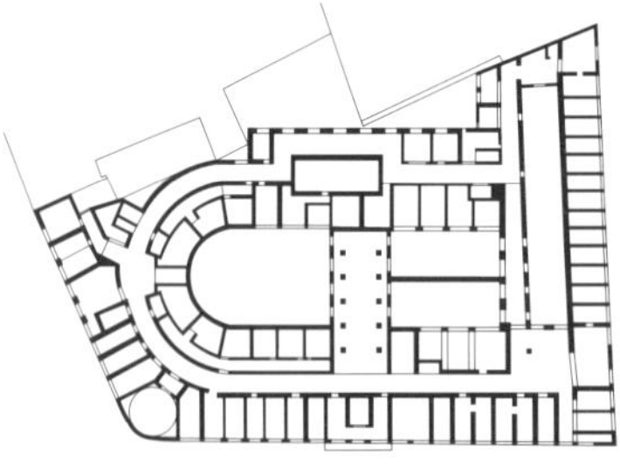

© Alf Hermann

architect
Fritz Schumacher

type
offices

construction
1914 1926

08. Große Bleichen 19

Große Bleichen 19
20354 Hamburg

open to the public

U1/U2/U4
Jungfernstieg

S1/S2/S3
Jungfernstieg

This intervention concerns an area in the heart of the historic center alongside the Old Post Office between Große Bleichen and Bleichenfleet. The building is six stories high with a total floor area of 6,700 square meters. The ground floor contains two retail areas, one facing the street, and the other overlooking the canal. The upper floors are composed of flexible rental office spaces, with natural lighting from a system of light wells in the central part of the building.

The building materials were chosen to harmonize with the existing adjacent facades, while certain details like the horizontal anodized aluminum bands, and the height variations of the upper windows underline the subtle interruptions that accentuate the contemporary design.

The relationship with the adjacent building, the historic Old Post Office, is visible in the choice of materials as well as in the alignments on the facades, and the thickness of the string courses and the eaves.

© TCHOBAN VOSS Architekten

© Axel Neubauer

architects
TCHOBAN VOSS Architekten

type
offices, commercial

construction
2018

09. Hamburger Rathaus

Rathausmarkt 1
20095 Hamburg

January - December
Mon - Sun / 7 am - 8 pm

+49 (0)40 428312064
www.hamburg.de/rathaus

U3
Rathaus

3/31/601/609/610
17/34/37/607/608/
641/X35
4/5/19/36/603/604/
605
Rathausmarkt

Built in neo-Renaissance style between 1886 and 1897, on the design of a team of architects led by Martin Haller, the Hamburg Town Hall (Hamburger Rathaus) replaced a previous building destroyed in the great fire of 1842. After World War II bombings, it was partly rebuilt in the 1950s. Today it is the seat of the land's government or the Senate of Hamburg and the Hamburg Parliament.

The granite and sandstone building is supported by 4,000 oak piles. Its facade is 111-meter wide and has a compositional and decorative system featuring lavish ornamental style in contrast with Hanseatic style. In addition to its moldings, tympanum, and spires, it has a large, 112-meter high tower on whose base there is a balcony topped with a mosaic of Hammonia, Hamburg's patron goddess. The internal courtyard has a fountain with Hygeia, goddess of health, in memory of the 1892 cholera epidemic. Among the 647 rooms inside, the emperor's room, Senate meeting room, and ballroom are the most impressive for their size and beauty.

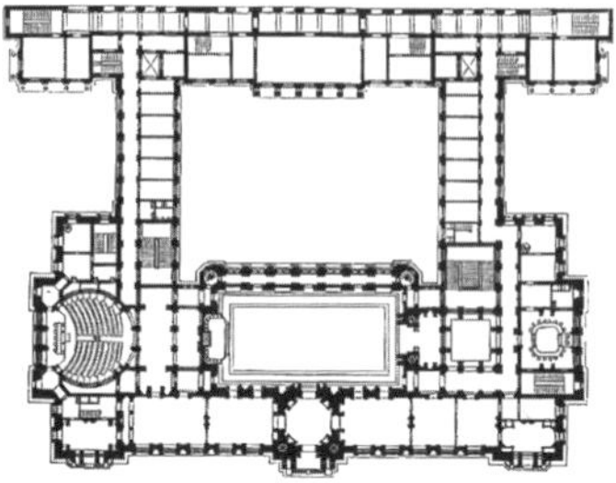

architect
Martin Haller

type
town hall

construction
1886-1897

10. Handelskammer Hamburg

Adolphsplatz 1
20457 Hamburg

January - December
Mon - Thu / 9 am - 4 pm
Fri / 10 am -3 pm
Sat - Sun / closed

+49 (0)40 36138138
www.hk24.de

U3
Rathaus

34/37/X35
U Rödingsmarkt
(Großer Burstah)

The building was built in 1840 on the design of architects Carl Ludwig Wimmel and Franz Gustav Joachim Forsmann on the former site of the monastery of St. Mary Magdalene. Until 1999, it was home to Hamburg Stock Exchange, the first in Germany founded in 1558 sited near Trosbrücke. The building is now home to the Chamber of Commerce. It is set behind the Hamburger Rathaus to which it is connected by a courtyard.

The building's layout and elements have touches of classical architecture style. It faces the city with a symmetrical main facade based on a projecting central structure organized on two twin rows. One holds an arcade and the other a terrace paced by columns framing arched openings, and two side arcades, set back from the first one.

It was saved from the 1842 fire by the merchants themselves and was expanded in 1859, 1880, and 1909. It has recently undergone major expansion and interior remodeling.

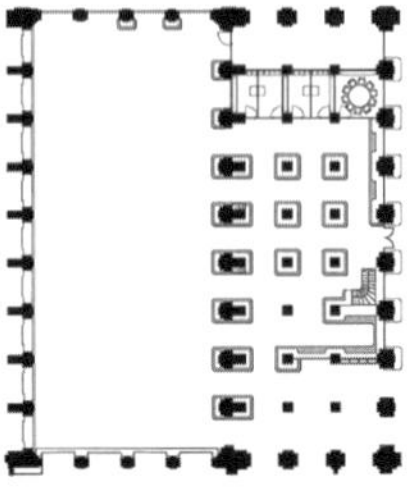

architects
Carl Ludwig Wimmel,
Franz Gustav Joachim
Forsmann

type
offices

construction
1840

11. Haus im Haus

Adolphsplatz 1
20457 Hamburg

January - December
Mon - Thu / 9 am - 4 pm
Fri / 10 am -3 pm
Sat - Sun / closed

U3
Rathaus

31
Großer Burstah

Hamburg's Chamber of Commerce has been a hub of economic life throughout the city's history. At the dawn of the new millennium, it required more intensive use than the existing neo-Classical building could accommodate. Plans started to design a new building to accommodate a business start-up space, a consultation center, an exhibition room, and meeting room, as well as access to roof terraces.

Respecting the existing structure, the design proposed placing inside of it a lightweight structure in contrast with the historic building's stonework. This "house within a house" provides 1,000 new square meters on five floors. This leaves free much of the large hall where the structure is placed. It preserves the place's spatial qualities through the use of bright, transparent and reflective materials that create an impression of lightweight immateriality, heightened by LED-based lighting developed by the architects jointly with members of Nimbus Design. The new expansion serves as a prism through which the historic hall can be seen from different perspectives.

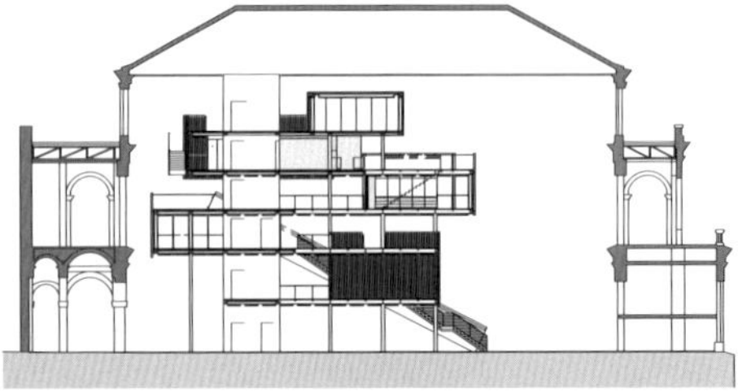

architects
Behnisch Architekten

type
offices, exhibition, restaurant

construction
2004-2007

12. JohannisContor

Große Johannisstraße 19
20457 Hamburg

external view only

U3
Rathaus

3/31/602/609/610/X3
4/5/17/19/34/36/37/
607/608/641/X35
Rathausmarkt

This grand office building is in the immediate vicinity of the City Hall and Chamber of Commerce. Its historic facades have been preserved facing the Große Johannisstraße, the Börsenbrücke and the Große Bäckerstraße and its interiors have been completely renovated. After gutting the existing building, eight floors were built in its interior and supported by a new reinforced concrete structure.

Restoration work on the facades and replacement of the wooden frames was joined by a major new construction that added a basement level, a ground floor with a 7-meter tall entrance lobby, two shops with an upper gallery for each one and six upper floors for offices. The office floors open onto the building's entire depth. They have a free composition and fantastic views outside.

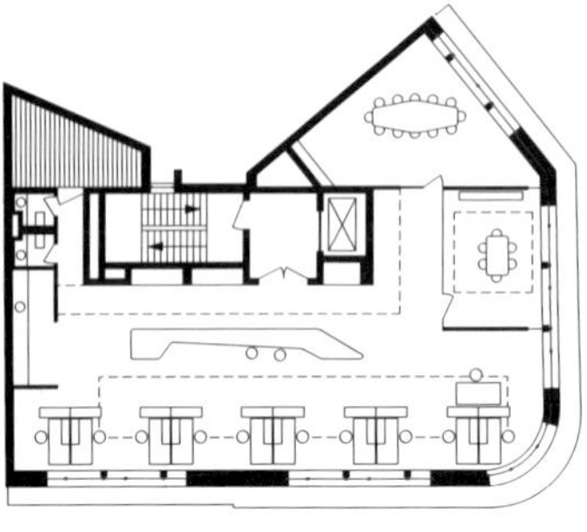

© Matteo Moscatelli

architects
KBNK Architekten

type
offices, commercial

construction
2008-2009

13. Mahnmal St. Nikolai

Willy-Brandt-Straße 60
20457 Hamburg

April - September
Mon - Sun / 10 am -6 pm
October - March
Mon - Sun / 10 am - 5 pm

+49 (0)40 371125
www.mahnmal-st-nikolai.de

U3
Rödingsmarkt

3/17/34/37/601/ 607/ 608/609/610/ 641/X35
U Rödingsmarkt
(Großer Burstah)

The ruins of the Mahnmal St. Nikolai (church of St. Nicholas) are now a memorial to the victims of World War II and the dictatorship imposed on Germany from 1933 to 1945, they show themselves to the city particularly through the tall tower whose spire soars to 147.3 meters. It was the tallest in the world when it was built and now has dropped to fifth place in the international rankings.

The basilica has three naves in neo-Gothic style. It was built between 1846 and 1874 on George Gilbert Scott's design in the place where the original church was destroyed by fire in 1842. It was the tall spire that inadvertently led to the city's ruin, though it survived the devastating destruction itself. Because it was the tallest edifice on the city's landscape, it became the main target for British bombers who chose it as a landmark in the night during 1943 bombings. Since 1951 a long debate on the possibility of rebuilding it led to a choice to conserve its ruins as a place of commemoration. The crypt is now home to a historic museum. The tower holds the fascination carillon from 1993 made of 51 bells and lets visitors climb up its 76 meters from which they can admire a panoramic view of the harbor, the River Alster, and Hamburg.

© Alf Hermann

architect
George Gilbert Scott

type
museum

construction
1846-1874

14. Steckelhörn 11

Steckelhörn 11
20457 Hamburg

external view only

U1
Meßberg
U3
Rödingsmarkt

4/6/602
Brandstwiete
6/602
Bei St. Annen

The Steckelhörn 11 project is near the new HafenCity development. Wedged between two historic buildings, it replaces a ruined older building. The triangular lot extends for the block's entire length. Its narrow facade, only 1.3 meters wide, is on the harbor side and the main long facade, about 26.4 meters, is on the Steckelhörn side. The triangular lot extends for the block's entire length. Its narrow facade, only 1.3 meters wide, is on the harbor side and the main long facade, about 26.4 meters, is on the Steckelhörn side.

The floor plan's unique shape defines its composition. The ground floor serves as a spacious atrium for its residents as well as a public café. The upper floors feature ample, flexible office spaces, most of which have views of the church of St. Catherine or of HafenCity. The top floors have use of ample outdoor areas with balconies, porches, and a roof terrace affording a spectacular, sweeping view of Hamburg.

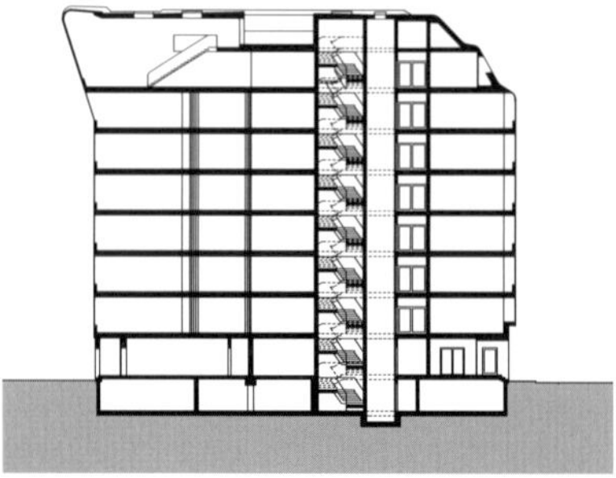

© Alf Hermann

architects
Jürgen Mayer H. und Partner, Architekten

type
offices

construction
2007-2009

15. Domplatz

Domstraße
20095 Hamburg

open to public

U3
Rathaus

4/6/602/X3
Rathausmarkt
(Petrikirche)

This temporary garden celebrates the resurrection of Hamburg's former Catholic church, the "Mariendom", demolished in the early nineteenth century. The grid arranged on the green lawn consists of forty white acrylic cushions that are lit from the inside. They let visitors sit and contemplate the past or just take a break from the city center's hub-bub.

Domburg's perimeter is outlined by fragments of a steel plate wall. A 140-meter high circular wall protected the former church before the city expanded. Remnants of it were uncovered by recent archeological excavations.

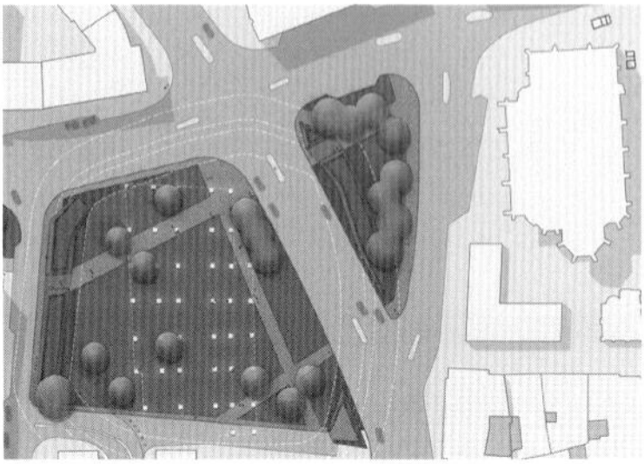

architects
Bruun & Möllers Landschaften

type
public space

construction
2009

16. Hamburger Kunsthalle

Glockengießerwall
20095 Hamburg

January - December
Tue - Sun / 10 am - 6 pm
Thu / 10 am - 9 pm
Mon / closed

+49 (0)40 428131200
www.hamburger-kunsthalle.de

U2/U4
Hauptbahnhof Nord

112
Kunsthalle

Hamburg's Kunsthalle is one of Germany's preeminent art museums. It consists of three buildings; one is a brick building built in 1869 by Georg Theodor Schirrmacher and Hermann von der Hude; another is a neo-Classical building from 1919 by the architects Albert Erbe and Fritz Schumacher; and the last is called the "Galerie der Gegenwart" designed by the architect Oswald Mathias Ungers.

The Galerie's volume rises on a massive red granite base. It is like a bastion to help separate the museum block from the city's chaos, adding a raised square under which there are exhibition and service spaces. The building is shaped on a square plan, 40 meters per side. It is clad externally by white limestone and inside it has a full-height central space closed by a glass skylight. A constant return to the square shape was typical of Ungers' work. Its aim is to define a pure image, evoking the classic origins of architecture made with strict proportions. This is evident in the construction of a minimalist structure with equal, white walls defined only by a series of windows marking the base level and central axes.

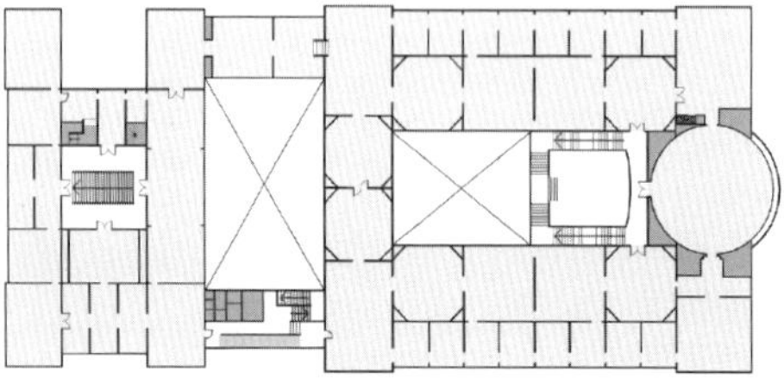

architect
Oswald Mathias Ungers

type
museum

construction
1986-1997

17. Commercial and Office Building on Lilienstraße

Lilienstraße 15
20095 Hamburg

external view only

U3
Mönckebergstraße

The building was designed for commercial and office space. Between 2003 and 2005, it was reorganized in terms of the distribution of its 3,500 square meters interior area and the external, street-side facade was completely renovated. The building originally featured a metal structure (maintained to support the new facade) and glazed bands along its width. The new facade has a massive quality and reintroduces the clinker tiles traditionally used in many of Hamburg's neighborhoods.

The facade's exterior on the building's eight levels has two overlapping patterns. For the first six floors, it is flush and has two bottom levels open with square windows. The four upper ones are made dynamic with five arches holding tripartite windows for every floor alternated with brick bands with patterns based on light and shadow effects. The facade on the top two floors, the penthouses, covers two floors set back from the one below it. They have close-set bands of windows, which let them be aligned with adjacent buildings, and lightens the top compared to its overall massive structure.

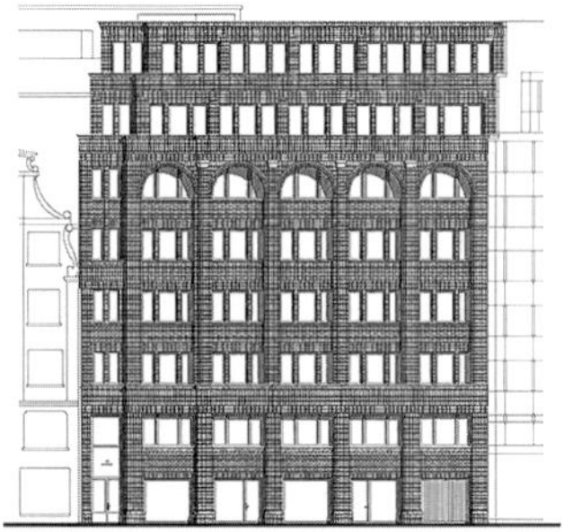

architects
Hans Kollhoff,
Helga Timmermann

type
commercial, offices

construction
2003-2005

18. Chilehaus

Fischertwiete 2
20095 Hamburg

access by appointment

www.chilehaus.de

U1
Meßberg

X3
U Meßberg

The Chilehaus building complex was built between 1922 and 1924 on the design of the German architect Fritz Höger; it counts ten floors and three internal courtyards. The complex is a major example of expressionist architecture, covering about 6,000 square meters at the intersection of Pumpen and Niedernstraße. In addition to the use of bricks with a translucent surface (of which there are some 4.8 million), another point of particular interest is its form evoking a ship's prow with an overhanging roof and a long, curved facade that ends in a point forming the corner between the two streets. The complex's configuration suggests its origins, which were connected to the magnate Henry Brarens Sloman. After making his fortune trading in sodium nitrate with Chile, he decided to build a building in his city dedicated to Chile, evoking the many, long journeys by ship he took to reach it. From the roof terrace gives a view of the nearby River Elbe, reminiscent of the sea.

The local rooms are also worth a visit to admire the 1920s interior design details, including linoleum floors, mahogany doors, and brass handles.

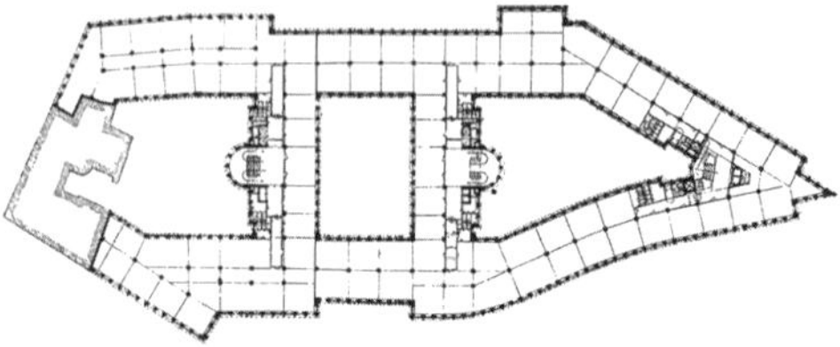

architect
Fritz Höger

type
offices

construction
1922-1924

19. Sprinkenhof

Burchardstraße 8
20095 Hamburg

limited access

www.sprinkenhof-hamburg.de

U1
Meßberg

X3
U Meßberg
X35
U Steinstraße

This majestic complex facing the Chilehaus, built between 1927 and 1943, is an impressive example of recently-restored expressionist architecture. The enormous construction is made up of the composition of several building structures supported by a reinforced concrete framework clad in brick. It appears compact from the outside and from the inside is broken into different areas divided by three large courtyards. The windows' regular grid outlined by white frames create a perpendicular grid on the dark brick wall face adorned by an ornamental pattern of oblique lines on the surface forming diamonds with dots. It was designed by the artist Ludwig Kunstmann to symbolize commerce and craft. The aim seems to be to lessen the surface's solid appearance, giving it the look of a nailed fabric curtain.

Many architects were involved in building the Sprinkenhof. The central structure covers nine floors around the Springeltwiete (1927-1928). The West Wing (1930-1932) was built by the Gerson brothers with Fritz Höger. The Sprinkenhof's East Wing (1939-1943) was designed by the architect Höger.

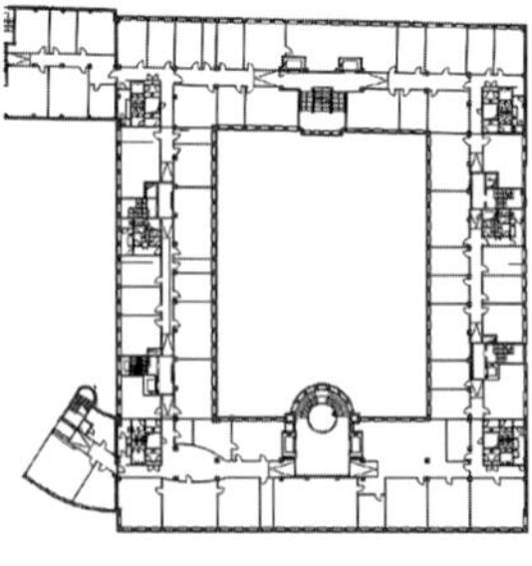

architects
Fritz Höger,
Hans and Oskar Gerson

type
offices, commercial

construction
1927-1943

20. DOC - Deichtor Office Center

Oberbaumbrücke 1
20457 Hamburg

external view only

deichtorofficecenter.de

U1
Meßberg

X3
U Meßberg

Located at the city's southern entrance, the Deichtor office building is a new landmark for Hamburg, set at the point of convergence between the "city" district, the Speicherstadt, and HafenCity. This location renders the building a point of mediation between the chaos of the street and railway and the calm of the canals' water.

The design's defining element is an alternation between the offices floors organized in a Z-form closed by reflecting facades. This composition creates empty spaces up to four floors high.

Four winter gardens and two large atria create green "windows" that enliven the building and create a comfortable indoor atmosphere, drawing attention from the outside at night and in the day. For acoustic and climate control reasons, the building is within a glass skin that allows excellent natural ventilation inside the offices. This considerably lowers heating and ventilation costs compared to conventional buildings.

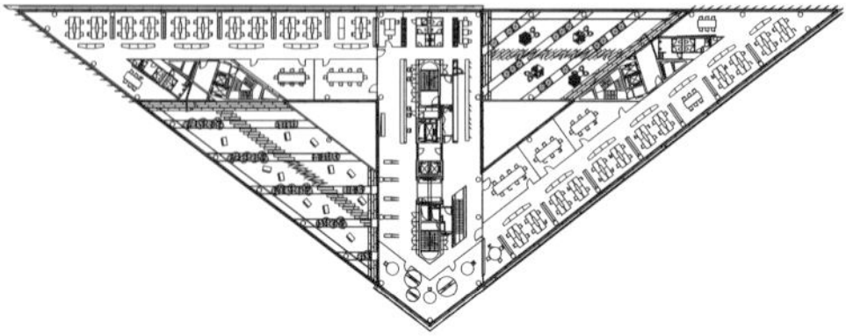

architects
Jens Bothe, Kai Richter,
Hadi Teherani

type
offices

construction
2000-2002

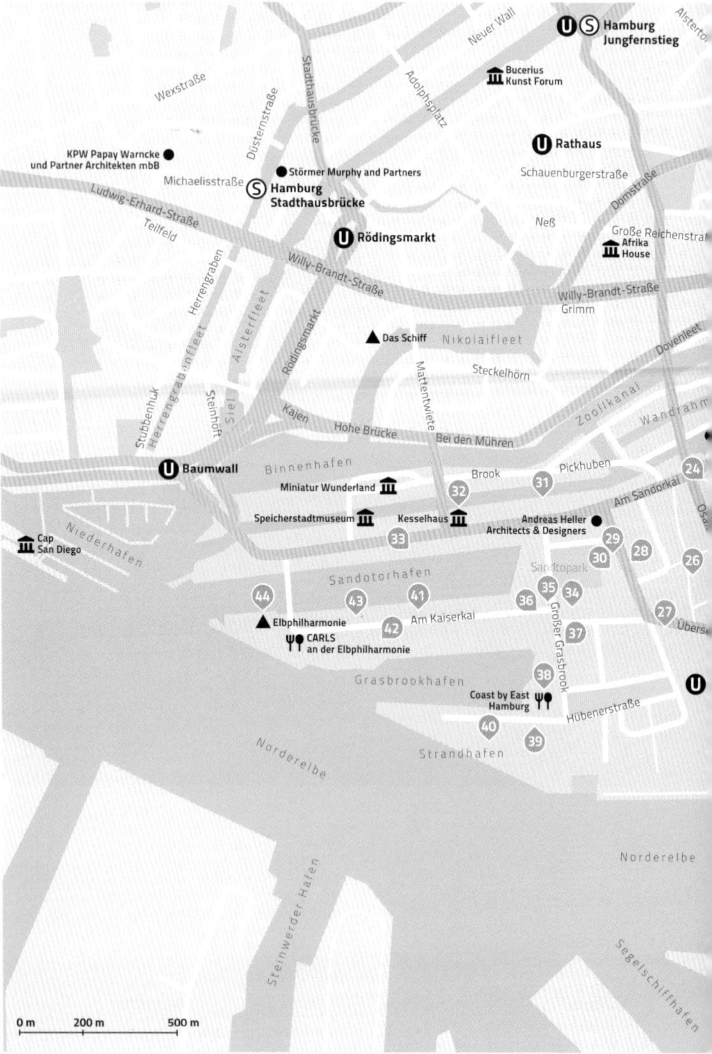

Hamburg Jungfernstieg
Neuer Wall
Alstertor
Bucerius Kunst Forum
Wexstraße
Stadthausbrücke
Adolphsplatz
Düsternstraße
Rathaus
KPW Papay Warncke und Partner Architekten mbB
Störmer Murphy and Partners
Schauenburgerstraße
Michaelisstraße
Hamburg Stadthausbrücke
Domstraße
Ludwig-Erhard-Straße
Teilfeld
Neß
Rödingsmarkt
Große Reichenstraße
Afrika House
Herrengraben
Willy-Brandt-Straße
Willy-Brandt-Straße
Grimm
Alsterfleet
Rödingsmarkt
Das Schiff
Nikolaifleet
Dovenfleet
Herrengrabenfleet
Mattentwiete
Steckelhörn
Stubbenhuk
Steinhöft
Siel
Zollkanal
Kajen
Hohe Brücke
Bei den Mühren
Wandrahm
Baumwall
Binnenhafen
Brook
Pickhuben
Miniatur Wunderland
Am Sandorkai
Speicherstadtmuseum
Kesselhaus
Andreas Heller Architects & Designers
Cap San Diego
Niederhafen
Sandtorhafen
Sandtorpark
Elbphilharmonie
Am Kaiserkai
Großer Grasbrook
CARLS an der Elbphilharmonie
Grasbrookhafen
Coast by East Hamburg
Hübenerstraße
Norderelbe
Strandhafen
Norderelbe
Steinwerder Hafen
Segelschiffhafen
0 m
200 m
500 m

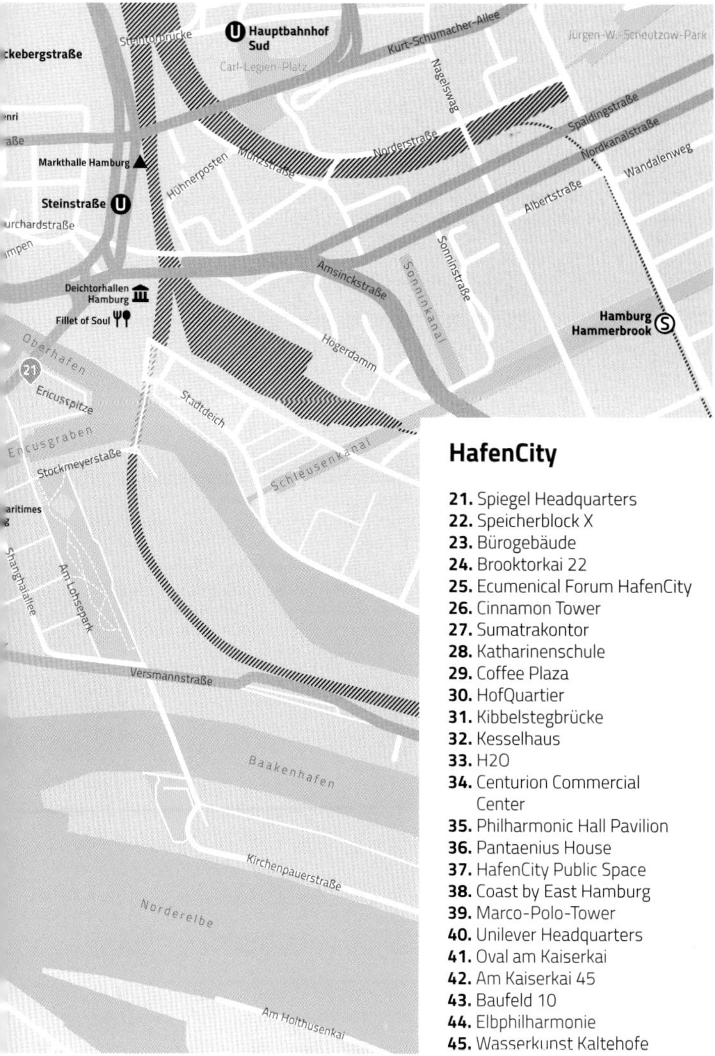

HafenCity

21. Spiegel Headquarters
22. Speicherblock X
23. Bürogebäude
24. Brooktorkai 22
25. Ecumenical Forum HafenCity
26. Cinnamon Tower
27. Sumatrakontor
28. Katharinenschule
29. Coffee Plaza
30. HofQuartier
31. Kibbelstegbrücke
32. Kesselhaus
33. H2O
34. Centurion Commercial Center
35. Philharmonic Hall Pavilion
36. Pantaenius House
37. HafenCity Public Space
38. Coast by East Hamburg
39. Marco-Polo-Tower
40. Unilever Headquarters
41. Oval am Kaiserkai
42. Am Kaiserkai 45
43. Baufeld 10
44. Elbphilharmonie
45. Wasserkunst Kaltehofe

21. Spiegel Headquarters

Ericusspitze 1
20457 Hamburg

external view only

+49 (0)40 301080
www.spiegel.de

U1
Meßberg

X3
U Meßberg

Located in the area known as 'Ericusspitze', joining HafenCity and Speicherstadt, the new headquarters of Der Spiegel publishing group is made up of two buildings; one is for the newspaper, and the other, called Ericus, accommodates other offices as well. The complex's considerable size (covering 50,000 square meters) make it a genuine urban icon.

Its design concept is based on optimal sustainability and energy efficiency, and it seeks to integrate the interior and exterior with a transparent skin that makes the workspaces visible. Those spaces, in turn, face surrounding public spaces through a monitor-like window carved out between the third and twelfth floors. On the outside, the Spiegel building surrounds an internal courtyard crossed by ramps at different levels. The Ericus opens towards Lohsepark, and both buildings face Brooktorkai and the riverfront.

From the outside, there is a noteworthy contrast with the solid base in burnished clinker and the upper volume in lightweight glass. Inside, there is a cafeteria in a triple-height space whose textures, colors, and Pop decor evoke (and partly reuse) those designed in 1969 by the designer Varner Panton for Spiegel's previous headquarters.

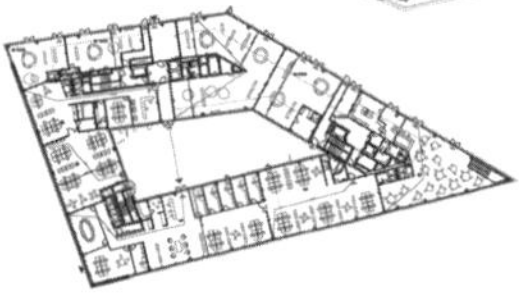

architects
Henning Larsen Architects

type
offices

construction
2008-2011

22. Speicherblock X

Brooktorkai 1
20457 Hamburg

external view only

U1
Meßberg

X3
U Meßberg

Though in 1910 an architectural project had been developed for this site, it remained unfinished until the start of the new millennium. At that point, a new office building was defined, extending the line of warehouses with a building of the same depth, height, compositional layout, and material use. This completed the Speicherstadt's set of buildings.

The central tower was originally planned with a tympanum at its peak. It was reconsidered with a modern approach and an asymmetrical brick facade paced by windows and vertical openings of varying widths, along with a horizontal division visible on the level of the roof structures. These structures were set above the eave line and the base, accommodating a parking lot and designed to protect against flooding at high tides.

The grand internal stairway is particularly interesting. In addition to serving the usual function, it is a small courtyard with a magnificent view of the Deichtormarkt.

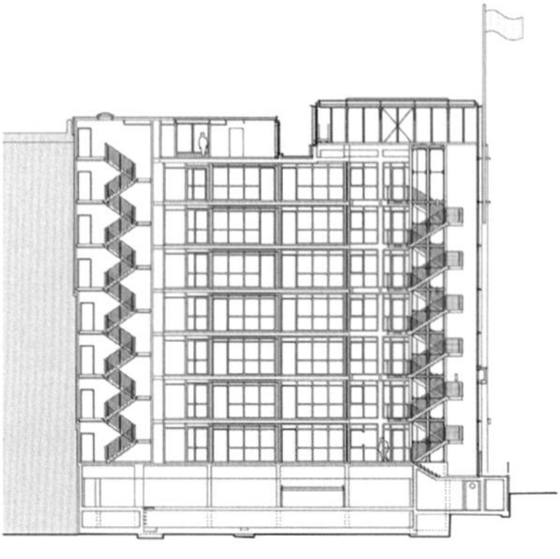

architects
gmp Architekten von Gerkan, Marg und Partner

type
offices

construction
2001-2002

23. Bürogebäude

Brooktorkai 20
20457 Hamburg

external view only

U1
Meßberg

602
Koreastraße

The new headquarters of the German firm Germanischer Lloyd is located in three different parts of the Brooktorkai area. The designs share their basic plan, snaking to create courtyard spaces open towards the canal or the historic Speicherstadt. They also share a tower with different claddings, becoming a landmark for each building. There also share an adjacent seven-floor building clad entirely in brick.

The current design is conceived as an independent unit with its own entrance and access to the underground parking lot. The tower building is clad with metal panels of pre-patinated copper, shaped into more than 80 different sizes. They alternate, according to the vantage point, between solids and semi-transparent grid pieces. Most of the interior finishes were made jointly with Germanischer Lloyd's Organization Department.

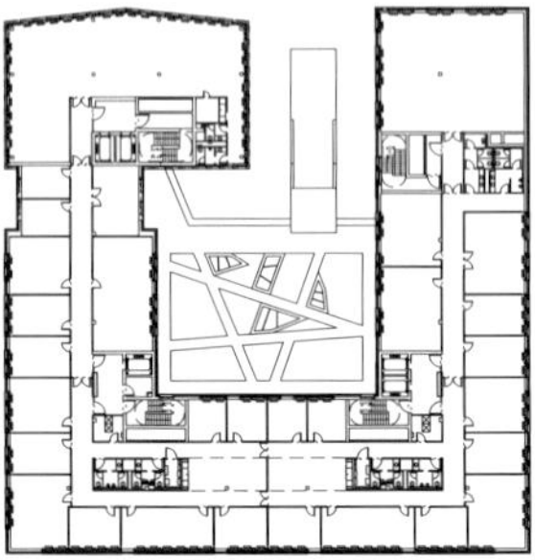

architects
Störmer Murphy and Partners

type
offices

construction
2005-2010

24. Brooktorkai 22

Brooktorkai 18-22
20457 Hamburg

ground floor access only

U1
Meßberg

602
Koreastraße

The building combines residential, commercial, and service functions in a single complex organized in two separate volumes sharing a glazed ground floor, projected towards the city's space. Within are a restaurant, a cafe, and differing entrance lobbies for offices or apartments.

The apartments are in the tower and afford an excellent view of the future open space of Lohsepark. Each apartment has a porch and windows with acoustic screening. Two penthouses on the top floor enjoy a sweeping view of Hamburg. The horizontal building is exclusively for offices.

The project's two sections face the city with two facades that are independent in terms of form, material, and colors. The austere, high residential building clad with large, irregularly-laid sandstone slabs and the dark red clinker of the horizontal office buildings are joined by the common feature of the bronze-color edging of the windows and glazings.

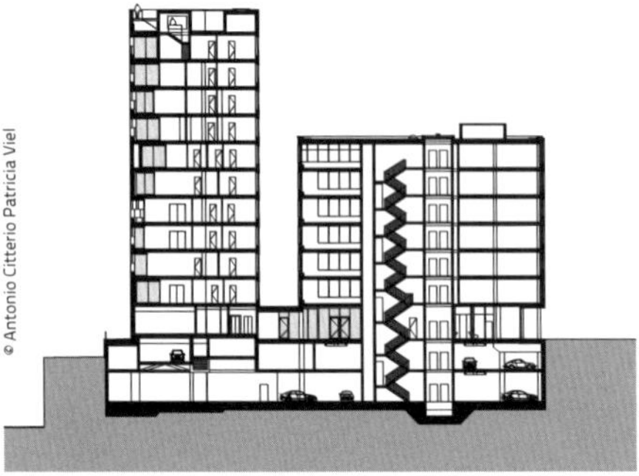

© Antonio Citterio Patricia Viel

architects
Antonio Citterio Patricia Viel

type
residential,
commercial, offices

construction
2005-2010

25. Ecumenical Forum HafenCity

Shanghaiallee 12
20457 Hamburg

Mon - Sun / 10 am - 6.30 pm

+49 (0)40 369002780
info@oefh.de
oekumenisches-forum-hafencity.de

U4
HafenCity Universität

602
Koreastraße; Shanghaiallee
111
Koreastraße

The Ecumenical Forum, is the first place of worship built in HafenCity, and overlooks Überseeallee between Lohsepark and the Magdeburger Bridge. It is composed of two buildings with different functions: one is an urban building for apartments and office space, discernible for its systematic layout and the horizontal and vertical alignment with surrounding buildings. The other is the religious building with facade variations created by a series of concave and convex contours on the long sides of the building.

The main facade on the street features two elements symbolic of Christian churches: a cross at ground floor level and a bell at the top of the building. Both elements are placed in concave recesses to underline their symbolic nature.

Red clinker brick was chosen to recall the industrial style of pre-existing buildings in the area. The bricks follow the lines of the curved facade, laid in co-planar style where the facade is rectilinear, and in staggered formation where it changes shape.

The facade design features regular repeated window and door openings aligned with those in adjacent buildings. On the ground floor the Ecumenical Forum houses a chapel, café, and information center, with offices and residential space on the upper floors.

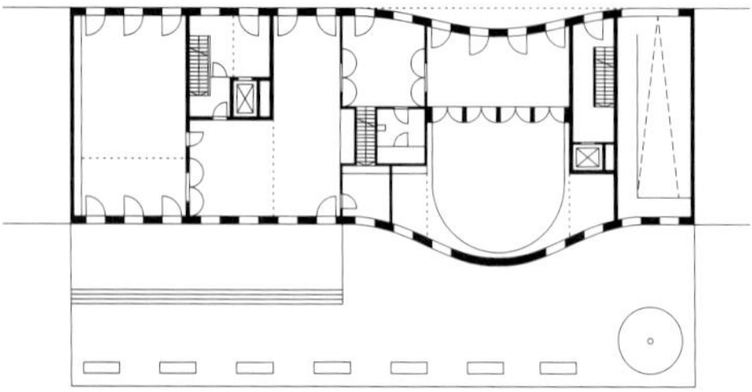

architects
Wandel Lorch Architekten

type
place of worship

construction
2010-2012

26. Cinnamon Tower

Osakaallee 10
20457 Hamburg

external viewing only

U4
Überseequartier

111
Osakaallee
6
Singapurstraße

The Cinnamon Tower overlooks the new Marktplatz square, at the point where the Überseeallee cuts diagonally across one of the major roads in the historic center. It is part of a large redevelopment scheme realized over several stages, which also includes the adjacent Harbor Masters Building and the Info Pavilion for the Überseequartier (Overseas Quarter).

A specific base/height ratio of one to four was used to create the slender line of this tall building, considered a fundamental aspect by the architects, plus a slight tapering of the facade from the eighth floor upwards to achieve a narrowing effect at the top of the tower. This configuration established the size and layout of the different apartments, based on duplex models with a few variations like the triplex apartment on the top floor and several one-floor units.

The openings on the south-east facade and the two adjacent sides help merge the interior with the exterior and, at the same time, expand the views over the adjoining river marina, while the opposite facade provides spectacular views of the new Elbphilharmonie Concert Hall. The facades are clad in anodized aluminum sheets in different gradations of dark red, coherent with those used on the neighboring pavilion built in 2008.

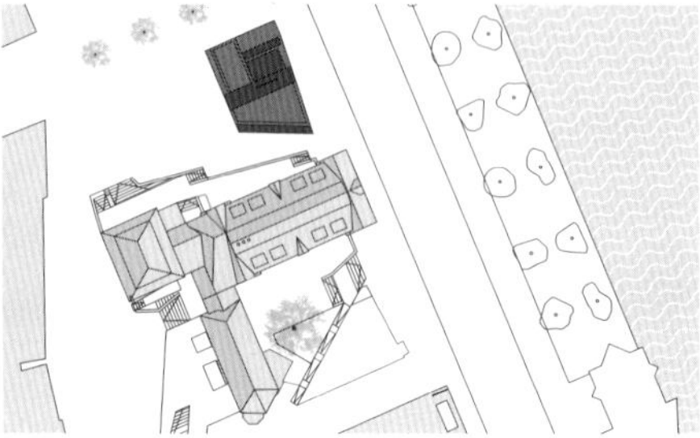

© BOLLES+WILSON

architects
BOLLES+WILSON

type
residential

construction
2013-2015

27. Sumatrakontor

Überseeallee 1
20457 Hamburg

external view only

U4
Überseequartier

111/602
U Überseequartier
111
Osakaallee

72
Elbphilharmonie

The building is also known as Überseequartier SPV 1-4 and is part of the like-named neighborhood on HafenCity's riverfront. The project covers an area of about 37,000 square meters. This large size and the facades' powerful character render it a major point of attraction in the city. The project includes shops on the ground floor and apartments and offices on the upper floors, overlooking the Überseeboulevard, a pedestrian connection between the inner-city and the River Elbe.

The architectural complex surrounds an inner courtyard. Its accessibility from the street makes it a semi-public space, intended for residents, but open to passers-by as well. The two-color facades face outwards and have variable heights that accentuate the vertical flight effect. Their lower part is clad in reddish stone evoking the Speicherstadt's typical buildings; the upper part, as well as the courtyard facades, are white with stucco, metal and glass, that are a reference to the city center's traditional plaster exteriors. The main entrance is at the opening slit that cuts a corner of the polygon.

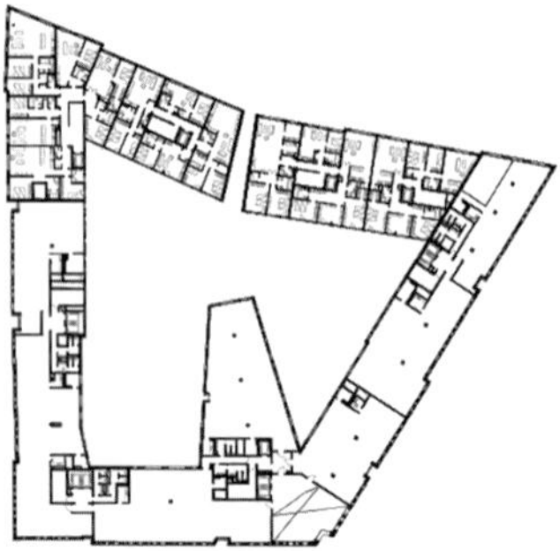

architects
Erick van Egeraat

type
residential, commercial, offices

construction
2007-2011

28. Katharinenschule

Am Dalmannkai 12-18
20457 Hamburg

external view only

U4
Überseequartier

111/602
U Überseequartier
111
Magellan-Terrassen

72
Elbphilharmonie

The first public building in the new HafenCity, located in the very dense urban area of Sandtorpark, is a hybrid complex of two buildings including a nursery, a primary school and some residences. The compact volume of the five-storey educational building is organized around a central lobby, surrounded by classrooms and a gym overlooking the lobby through large windows. The building's flat roof stretches around it and holds an original playground surrounded by a high wall rendered vibrant with tilted, colorful components. The building's nature is at once educational and playful, designed to be experienced, first and foremost, by children.

The windows marking the four outer facades are cut laterally with oblique lines that help display the building's character. An essential feature is the design's use of materials and color. The school's common spaces feature strong colors, giving way to the white for the classrooms and hallways. The facade is covered with lightweight beige and gray bricks.

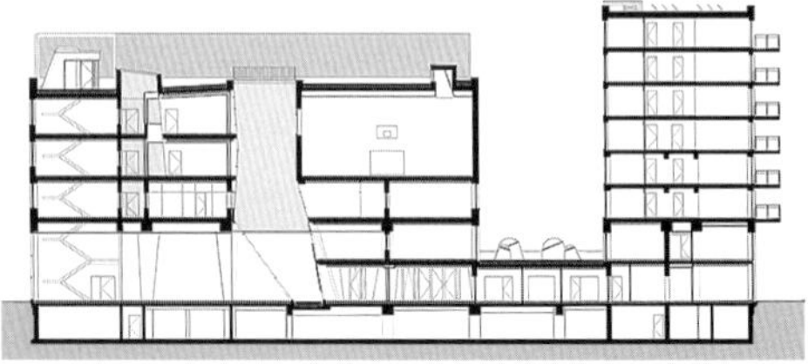

architects
Spengler Wiescholek

type
primary school,
nursery, residential

construction
2007-2009

29. Coffee Plaza

Am Sandtopark 2-6
20457 Hamburg

open to public

U4
Überseequartier

111/602
U Überseequartier
111
Magellan-Terrassen

72
Elbphilharmonie

The three-building complex is located near the Magellan-Terrassen. One of the buildings is the headquarters of a world-leading coffee trading firms; the other two are for offices and include rentable spaces, a public square, and an underground parking. The main tower has an oval plan and is set on a podium directly overlooking Sandtorpark. It is 12 floors high, eleven of which are for offices and the last of which has a penthouse with conference rooms and a breathtaking view of the city.

Mechanical systems and facade technologies were meticulously designed to minimize the building's energy use. For example, the southern and western walls are shaded by vertical glass slits that rotate in response to the sunlight.

The building complex and square's relationships with the urban setting is vital, creating a sculptural form that defines the place, conceived as a hub of city life.

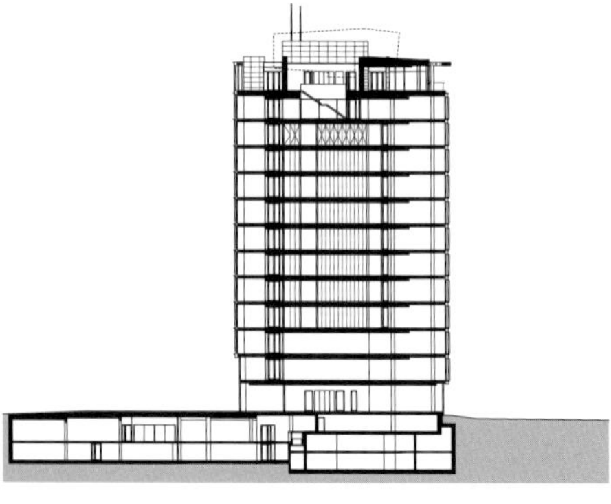

architects
Richard Meier
& Partners Architects

type
public space,
commercial, offices

construction
2004-2010

30. HofQuartier

Am Sandtorpark 8
Am Dalmannkai 10
20457 Hamburg

external view only

U4
Überseequartier
U3
Baumwall
(Elbphilharmonie)

111
Magellan-Terrassen

72
Elbphilharmonie

The HofQuartier residential building is adjacent to a primary school in the HafenCity. It is in a L-shape that tapers on its longer axis to maintain a distance from the school.

The ground floor, which has a primarily commercial use, and the top floor are distinguished by their surfaces and colors from the rest of the building, from which they are set back. The upper floors hold 42 apartments with flexible floor plans, designed to keep a fixed core of services around which each apartment can be organized to fit its inhabitants' needs. So a variation of layouts can be realized, from an open loft-type arrangement to a family friendly layout with several rooms.

The facade and roof systems are highly insulating. Controlled ventilation and the use of durable materials make the building very sustainable and inexpensive to operate.

architects
KBNK Architekten

type
residential

construction
2010

31. Kibbelstegbrücke

Kibbelsteg
20457 Hamburg

open to public

U4
Überseequartier

6/111
Am Sandtorkai
6/602
Singapurstraße

72
Elbphilharmonie

A short ways from the information center on the Speicherstadt, the new Kibbelsteg Bridge connects HafenCity and the historic center.

In keeping with the Speicherstadt's historic bridges, built between the nineteenth and twentieth centuries with a lattice arch structure, the Kibbelsteg Bridge uses the same construction method, to this day an economically and structurally sound solution.

The bridge was designed to connect different levels of the two banks. As the structure has two stonework points of support, it consists of two stacked walkways, bound by two lattice arch structures giving it a distinctive form, perfectly fitting into its urban setting, which is now under historical monument protection regulation.

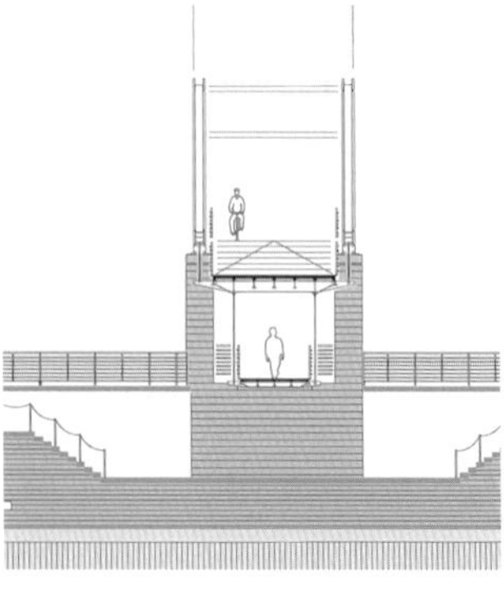

architects
gmp Architekten von Gerkan, Marg und Partner

type
bridge

construction
2001-2002

32. Kesselhaus

Am Sandtorkai 30
20457 Hamburg

October - April
Tue - Sun / 10 am - 6 pm
Mon / closed
May - September
Tue - Sun / 10 am - 6 pm
Thu / 10 am - 8 pm
Mon / closed

U4
Überseequartier
U3
Baumwall
(Elbphilharmonie)

6/111
Am Sandtorkai

72
Elbphilharmonie

HafenCity's new information center is in Hamburg's former thermal power station, which was its first steam power plant, recently converted to new uses. The power station had been in operation since 1888, set in the Speicherstadt, a historic complex of 17 warehouses built between 1884 and 1888 on the design of Franz Andreas Meyer, an engineer from Hamburg. No longer in use, it was declared a protected monument in 1991.

The building is neo-Gothic and maintains its original structure with an oak wood foundation and red brick walls. Its abstract building envelope with two 20 meters high chimneys suggests the building's historic origins from the outside. The ample size of its rooms inside makes way for new functions. The ground floor on the western part is used as a foyer. The central building is an exhibition hall and holds the HafenCity model. It is 300 meters long and closed on top by a truss ceiling creating an interesting steel lattice structure.

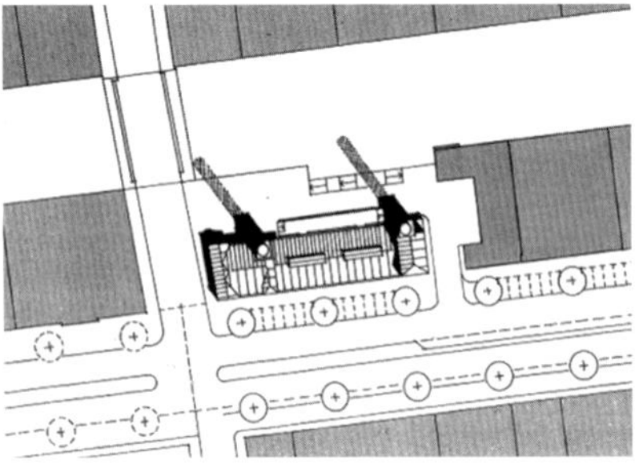

architects
gmp Architekten von Gerkan, Marg und Partner

type
info center

construction
2000-2001

33. H2O

Am Sandtorkai 64
20457 Hamburg

external view only

The building, used for apartments and offices, juxtaposes a main structure anchored to the ground and two rectangular structures, projecting towards the canal, set crossways to the first building, forming a C layout. Its dual purpose requires flexibility in the spaces internal composition and is made visible from the outside by a calibration of the windows and different surface treatments at the levels of the apartments and workspaces. The facades give highlight the glazed curtains supported by diagonal metal components for the offices and more closed, brick-clad surfaced for the apartments' more private areas. The entire building has technological systems for optimal energy savings.

The apartments are of different sizes and have bay windows overlooking the sea. The apartments on the upper floors have attractive winter gardens on the flat roofs.

U4
Überseequartier
U3
Baumwall
(Elbphilharmonie)

6/111
Am Sandtorkai
111
Am Kaiserkai
(Elbphilharmonie)

72
Elbphilharmonie

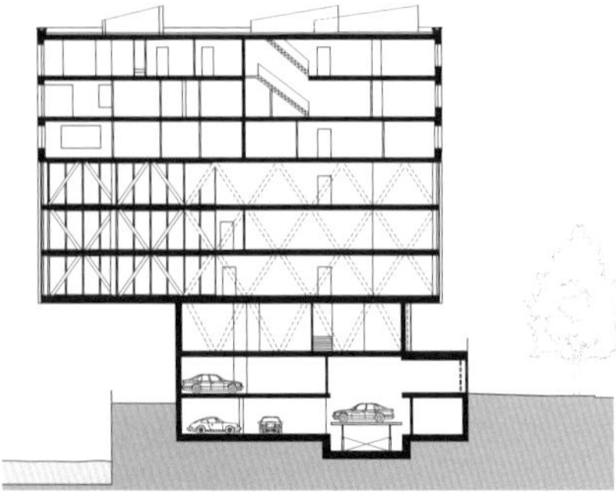

© Spengler Wiescholek

architects
Spengler Wiescholek

type
residential, offices

construction
2003-2005

34. Centurion Commercial Center

Großer Grasbrook 9
20457 Hamburg

open to the public

U4
Überseequartier

111/602
Magellan-Terrassen;
U Überseequartier

This project was inspired by the industrial architectural style of the buildings that previously occupied this area of the port, and recalls the design, based on a plain simple configuration and neutral style.

Together with the building by David Chipperfield, which stands on the opposite side of the street, this structure between Grasbrookhafen and Sandtorhafen marks the entrance to the neighboring residential and office building complexes in the southern part of the new HafenCity.

The facade features a system of glass sun shield panels that filter the light through their translucent surface. The internal layouts are inspired by traditional Hamburg office buildings. The meeting rooms directly overlook two central courtyards, flooding the internal spaces with natural light. The main materials, wood and natural stone, were chosen for their hard-wearing durability, given the high traffic foreseen in common areas. Flexible layout concepts in work areas permit the possibility of different configurations for future needs.

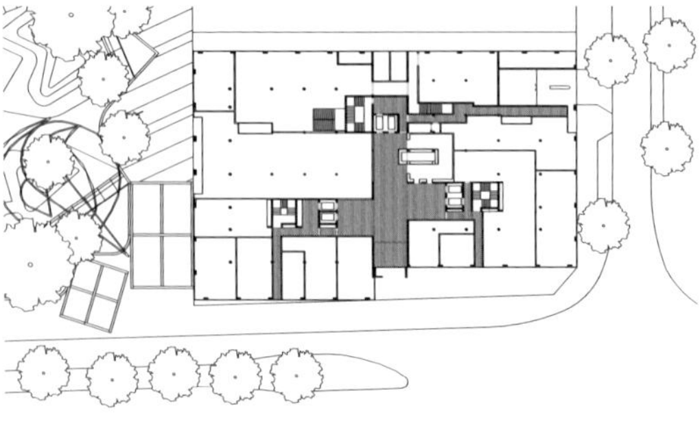

architects
Baumschlager Eberle
Architekten

type
mixed use building

construction
2009-2010

35. Philharmonic Hall Pavilion

Großer Grasbrook
20457 Hamburg

open to public

The pavilion is in HafenCity's main square, the Magellan-Terrassen, and is in direct line of sight with the Elbphilharmonie. It is made up of a steel structure that can be easily separated into parts, forming a 10×10×10 meter cube. The lower third of the structure is clad with steel plate on which visual and acoustic components are installed; the two upper thirds are clad in glass panes. Its natural light and artificial lighting effects make it appear as if the pavilion were wavering and floating on the square and water around it.

The building's ground floor features a central through corridor on whose side is the exhibition space for the Elbphilharmonie. There is a large hall on the first floor, which can be rented for events, conferences, and other purposes. Two side stairways give access the top floor.

On the top floor there is a 1:10 model of the Main Concert Hall, which was made to let eminent acoustics expert, Yasuhisa Toyota, perform experiments and measurements to optimize the hall's acoustics.

U4
Überseequartier
U3
Baumwall
(Elbphilharmonie)

602/111
Magellan-Terrassen

72
Elbphilharmonie

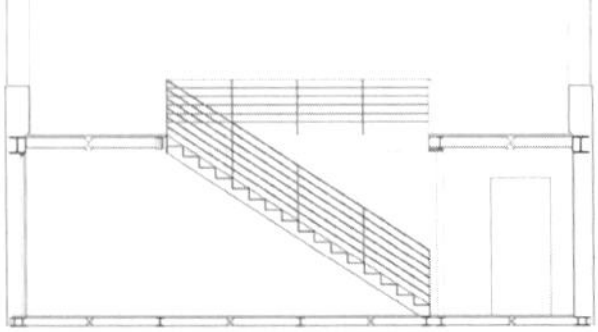

architects
Andreas Heller
Architects & Designers

type
theater, museum

construction
2008

36. Pantaenius House

Großer Grasbrook 10
20457 Hamburg

external view only

U4
Überseequartier

602/111
Magellan-Terrassen

72
Elbphilharmonie

The building is near the Speicherstadt at the far corner from the quay and is the headquarters of Pantaenius naval insurance company. The Pantaenius House is in a dominant city location. It has two structures of different heights arranged in an L plan: the shorter, six-story building faces the west towards the nearby residential buildings. The taller, eight-story, building faces the north shore and mainly holds offices.

The outside brick cladding unifies the building in a monolithic form, cut horizontally from north to south by long deep incisions of continuous windows and balconies. This creates openness to the outside while protecting the interiors from the Sun. The interiors feature powerful compositional flexibility, enhanced by the view towards the port that improves the working environment in each office.

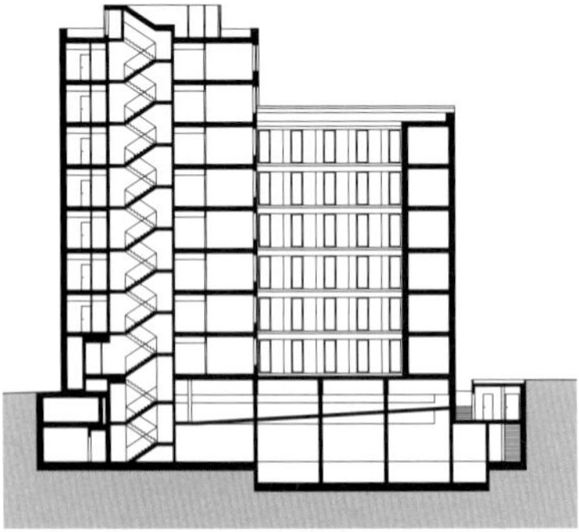

architects
David Chipperfield Architects

type
offices

construction
2002-2005

37. HafenCity Public Space

Großer Grasbrook
20457 Hamburg

open to public

U4
Überseequartier

111/602
Marco-Polo-Terrassen

72
Elbphilharmonie

This new public space is in HafenCity's eastern part. It was designed to give Hamburg's residents and visitors a place for recreation and relaxation along the former harbor wharf. It develops over several levels joined by a series of ramps, stairways and walkways. The area is shaped by the composition of natural and artificial elements placed in dialogue through their forms' fluidity. Stone pavement, wooden, stone and metal urban furnishing, green areas and pools of water are arranged in different combinations on each level, making for striking color variations in different seasons.

At the level on the water (0.00 m a.s.l.) there is a large floating platform to access small boats. The intermediate level (4.50 m a.s.l.) is for pedestrians and small cafes. The street level (7.50 m a.s.l.) includes rest and play areas as a filter between the canal and heavy traffic.

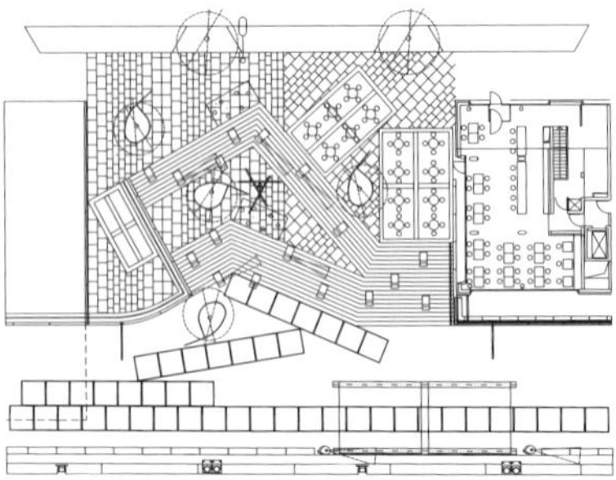

architects
Benedetta Tagliabue –
Miralles Tagliabue EMBT

type
public space

construction
2002-2014

38. Coast by East Hamburg

Großer Grasbrook 14
20457 Hamburg

Mon - Thu, Sun /
12 am - 10 pm
Fri - Sat / 12 am - 11 pm

+49 (0) 40 30993230
info@coast-hamburg.de
www.coast-hamburg.de

U4
Überseequartier

111/602
Marco-Polo-Terrassen

72
Elbphilharmonie

The Coast by East restaurant is close to the Marco-Polo-Tower in the western part of HafenCity in an area surrounded by a number of iconic buildings recently built as part of the urban redevelopment scheme. The building houses a restaurant with panoramic views, and stands out for its undulating roof shape, inspired by a seagull in flight. Both the roof surface and cross section have a curved profile repeated in the overall configuration and geometry of the individual structural modules.

The main restaurant is composed of a large open space surrounded by a long wall of tall glass windows facing Marco-Polo-Terrassen, the river harbor, and the new Elbphilharmonie Concert Hall. The opposite wall features a full-height vertical garden.

All structural elements and facings are in wood while the exterior has metal cladding in different colors. The roof over the entrance is designed as an element of transition between the restaurant and the outdoor space, and like other public areas in HafenCity, was created by the same architectural firm.

© Benedetta Tagliabue – Miralles Tagliabue EMBT

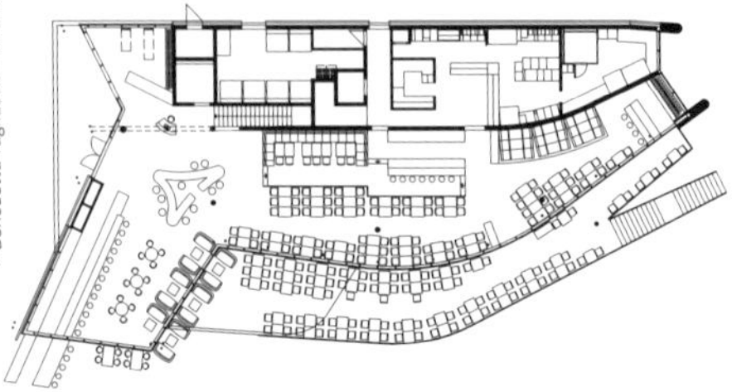

© Benedetta Tagliabue – Miralles Tagliabue EMBT

architects
Benedetta Tagliabue –
Miralles Tagliabue EMBT

type
restaurant

construction
2011-2014

39. Marco-Polo-Tower

Hübenerstraße 1
20457 Hamburg

external view only

U4
Überseequartier

111/602
Marco-Polo-Terrassen

72
Elbphilharmonie

The Marco-Polo-Tower is on the edge of the River Elbe and looms over HafenCity from its raised position near the Unilever offices designed by the same architects. The tower's 55 meters render it the culmination of a trajectory from the city center to the new district. Its original sculptural form makes it a landmark for the area, a distinctive feature of Hamburg's new skyline. Its 17 floors revolve around the tower's central axis, opening its 58 apartments to scenic views of the harbor and the city. The apartments vary between 60 and 340 square meters, ranging from simple one-bedroom apartments to multi-story penthouses. Each apartment has large terraces that are continuations of the living areas and offer protection from direct light for the facades under them.

The building was built using state-of-the-art technological systems. Its highly flexible design allows adjacent apartments to be joined into larger ones.

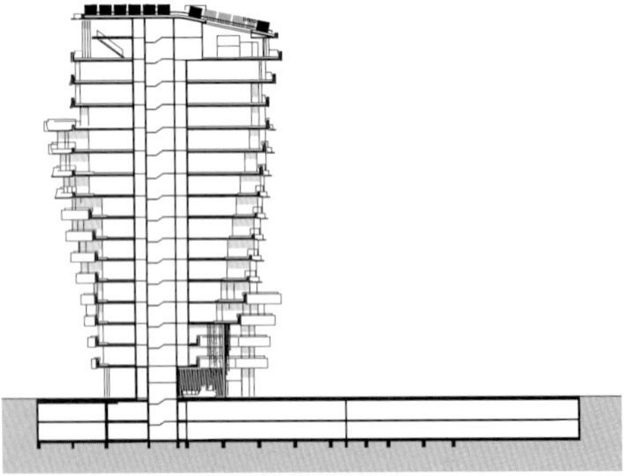

architects
Behnisch Architekten

type
residential

construction
2007-2010

40. Unilever Headquarters

Strandkai 1
20457 Hamburg

ground floor access only

U4
Überseequartier

111/602
Marco-Polo-Terrassen

72
Elbphilharmonie

The new headquarters of the multinational Unilever were designed next to the Marco-Polo-Tower, dominating HafenCity's skyline. The design was powerfully influenced by the nearby harbor. The building is shaped like a large glass ship stretching towards the canal. Its concept started from the two primary elements of light and transparency.

The external double envelope is made entirely of glass and metal. The space inside opens to the public with ample areas developing primarily in the large, full-height central atrium. The atrium, used for retail, is flooded with light from above and the side. The work spaces of the upper floors overlook the atrium. The spaces are on the levels above the side spaces of the central courtyard and linked through walkways and ramps.

The entire building is based on sustainable architecture principles to create an optimal microclimate in terms of temperature, acoustics, ventilation, and light.

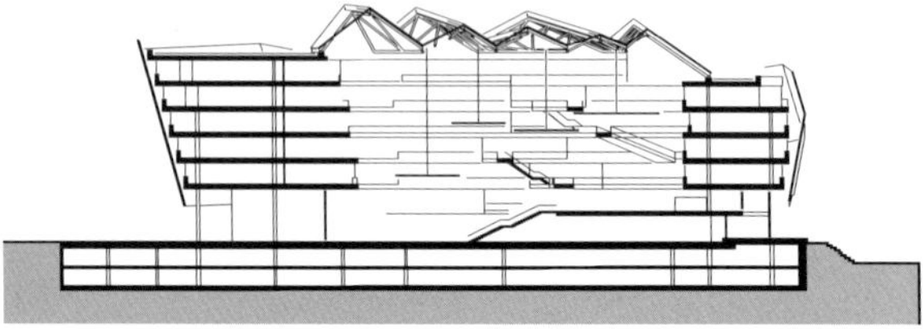

architects
Behnisch Architekten

type
commercial, offices

construction
2007-2009

41. Oval am Kaiserkai

Am Kaiserkai 12
20457 Hamburg

external view only

U4
Überseequartier

111/602
Magellan-Terrassen

72
Elbphilharmonie

This eleven-story residential tower is on Kaiserkai's northern shore in the new HafenCity district. Its location offers a magnificent view of Hamburg's center, the Speicherstadt, and the harbor. The complex has two buildings connected to each other underground. One is a horizontal rectangular building mainly for offices, and one is a tower with an oval plan for apartments. The glass facade was designed to undulate following the incidence of sunrays; its transparency is in contrast to the curved floor slabs that pace the ten stacked floors. The apartment tower is supported by six concrete columns set radially on the level of the building's ground floor. Its oval form is a distinguishing feature of the design and was developed by studying the site's prevailing wind conditions. The glass facade was also designed to undulate following the incidence of Sun rays; its transparency is in contrast to the curved floor slabs that pace the ten stacked floors.

Each of the tower's floors can hold up to three apartments in various combinations with sizes between 60 and 125 square meters.

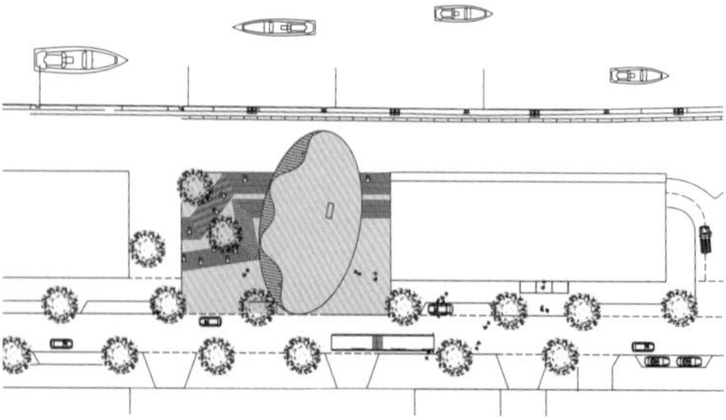

architects
Ingenhoven Architects

type
residential, offices

construction
2006-2008

42. Am Kaiserkai 45

Am Kaiserkai 45
20457 Hamburg

external view only

U4
Überseequartier

111/602
Magellan-Terrassen

72
Elbphilharmonie

Known as "VanMeer", the building evokes the area's port nature with an appearance of overlapping traditional containers. The alternation between white glass and red metal sets the pace of the floors. The five bands of metal cladding project from the main building, creating balconies and porches set in different directions, affording the 24 apartments beautiful views of the River Elbe.

The basement and ground floor are used for retail spaces, contrasting with a penthouse apartment including an office wing. The apartments on the intermediate floors have two or four bedrooms and areas from 65 to 150 square meters. The central stairway is of particular interest, developing in form and structure like a tree as if each floor were overlooking the landscape through a branch with a different rotation. Light dominates all the interiors and is bolstered by covering materials like wood, white plaster, and German Anröchter limestone.

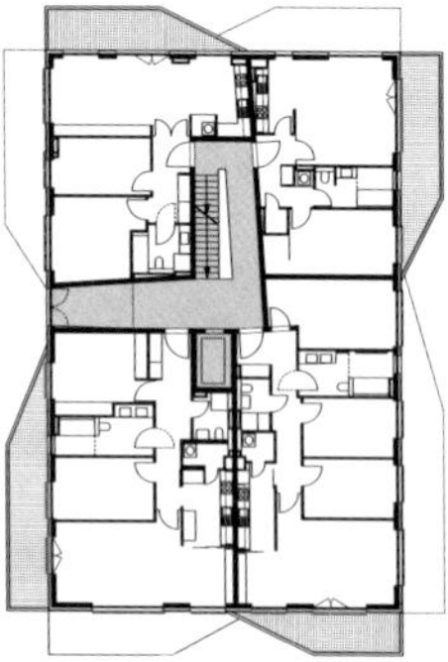

architects
SML Architekten Benedikt Schmitz + Maike Lück

type
residential, commercial

construction
2006-2007

43. Baufeld 10

Am Kaiserkai 56
20457 Hamburg

external view only

U4
Überseequartier

111/602
Magellan-Terrassen

72
Elbphilharmonie

The Baufeld 10 project includes 24 apartments, two retail spaces, and one restaurant. It was developed as a joint venture in collaboration with future residents united in a true community. Each family unit had the option of customizing its apartment, which created a complex of apartments that each differ in size (ranging from 50 to 225 square meters), composition and furnishing.

The outside of the building is homogeneous; its envelope serves as a heat insulation system made up of a wall structure covered in white natural stone powder with a mica addition, making the surface shine in the sunlight. The vertical walls feature prefabricated elements that give the facades their character. These slightly rounded, projecting cubes hold balconies and large glass windows following the apartments' layout. The windows are also rounded and afford a beautiful view of the harbor.

architects
LOVE architecture
and urbanism ZT GmbH

type
residential, commercial

construction
2007-2008

44. Elbphilharmonie

Platz der Deutschen Einheit
20457 Hamburg

access by appointment

+49 (0)40 35766666
pavillon@elbphilharmonie.de
www.elbphilharmonie-erleben.de

U3
Baumwall
(Elbphilharmonie)
U4
Überseequartier

111
Am Kaiserkai
(Elbphilharmonie)

72
Elbphilharmonie

This work in an overlapping of the existing Kaispeicher A warehouse, a compact brick building designed by Werner Kallmorgen and built between 1963 and 1966 with a new, soaring glass building rising to 108 meters. Hamburg's new Philharmonic is located at the Kaispitze, the tip of HafenCity's peninsula. It was conceived as an icon of the new city, visible from the outside and opening to a view of the River Elbe and its canals. The building is distinguished by a marked contrast between its two structures and the unusual undulating roof. Within is a concert hall seating 2,150 in a tiered arrangement facing the central orchestra. The pre-existing building mainly holds parking lots and an interactive music museum for children. The new building has a large hall surrounded by service areas, a theater, a cafe, restaurants, 45 apartments, and a 250-room hotel, conference hall and spa.

A raised square divides the solid part of the base volume from the one set on top, which is clad with 1,100 glass panels curved and individually cut to foster natural ventilation, stretching over an area equaling three soccer fields.

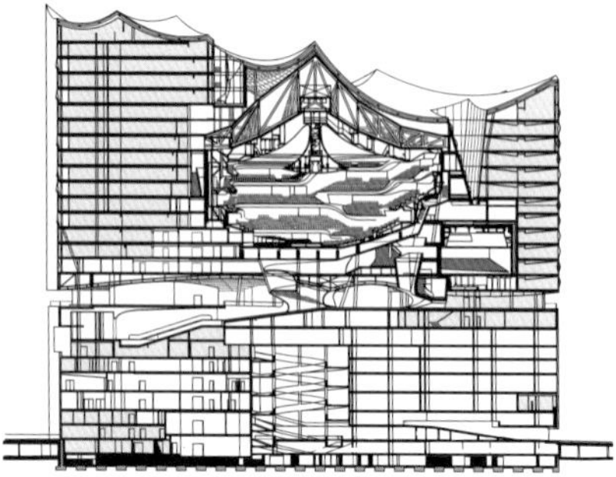

architects
Herzog & de Meuron

type
thealer

construction
2003-2017

45. Wasserkunst Kaltehofe

Kaltehofe Hauptdeich 6-7
20539 Hamburg

March - October
Mon - Sun / 10 am - 6 pm
November - February
Tue - Sun / 10 am - 6 pm

+49 (0)40 788849990
info@wasserkunst-hamburg.de
www.wasserkunst-hamburg.de

S2/S21
Tiefstack

530
Wasserkunst Kaltehofe; Kaltehofe-Hinterdeich

The redevelopment project for Kaltehofe Island on the River Elbe is a project by Hamburg Wasserwerke (Hamburg waterworks) and was part of the Agenda 21 on Environment and Development. The Agenda was initiated by Schutzgemeinschaft Deutscher Wald (SDW) environmental protection association, in order to preserve the natural environment, restoring the existing water filtering system and creating a nature routee enhanced by a local history museum and hydraulic engineering.

The project involved restoring and converting a historic villa from 1894 and building a new minimalist design building. Though in contrast to the historic villa, the new building subtly joined it, connecting through an underground tunnel. The building has a rectangular form and is closed externally by precast concrete elements whose abstract form suggests the pattern of the waterfall that falls in the surrounding pool.

The project is driven by sustainability and environmental conservation, is dedicated to using renewable energy, recycling waste and preserving the contrast between human-shaped nature and the wild environment in which 281 and 44 birds dwell.

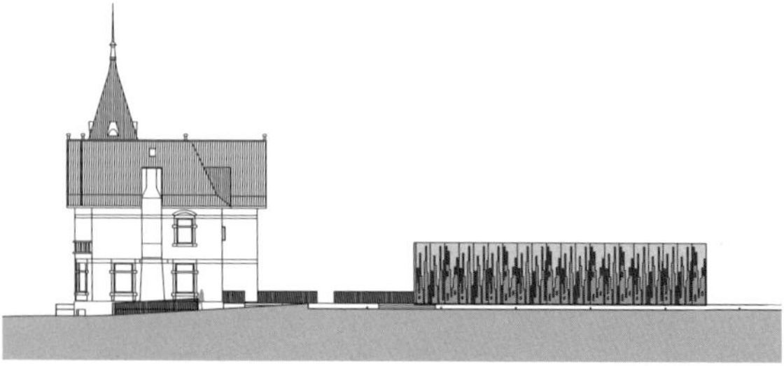

architects
Andreas Heller
Architects & Designers

type
museum, public space

construction
2010-2011

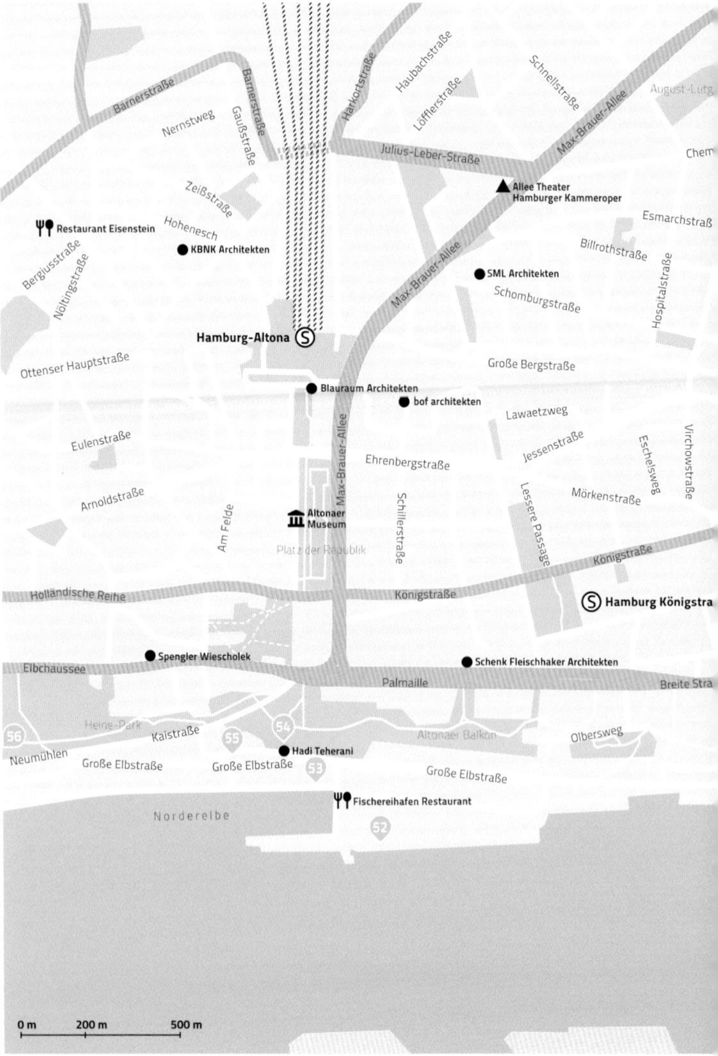
Barnerstraße
Nernstweg
Gaußstraße
Harkortstraße
Haubachstraße
Löfflerstraße
Schnellstraße
Max-Brauer-Allee
August-Lütg
Julius-Leber-Straße
Chem
Zeißstraße
Allee Theater
Hamburger Kammeroper
Esmarchstraß
Restaurant Eisenstein
Hohenesch
KBNK Architekten
Bergiusstraße
Nöltingstraße
Billrothstraße
Hospitalstraße
SML Architekten
Schomburgstraße
Hamburg-Altona
Ottenser Hauptstraße
Große Bergstraße
Blauraum Architekten
bof architekten
Lawaetzweg
Eulenstraße
Jessenstraße
Eschelsweg
Virchowstraße
Ehrenbergstraße
Arnoldstraße
Mörkenstraße
Lessere Passage
Schillerstraße
Altonaer Museum
Am Felde
Platz der Republik
Königstraße
Holländische Reihe
Hamburg Königstra
Spengler Wiescholek
Schenk Fleischhaker Architekten
Elbchaussee
Palmaille
Breite Stra
Heine-Park
Kaistraße
Altonaer Balkon
Olbersweg
56
55
54
53
52
Hadi Teherani
Neumühlen
Große Elbstraße
Fischereihafen Restaurant
Norderelbe
0 m
200 m
500 m

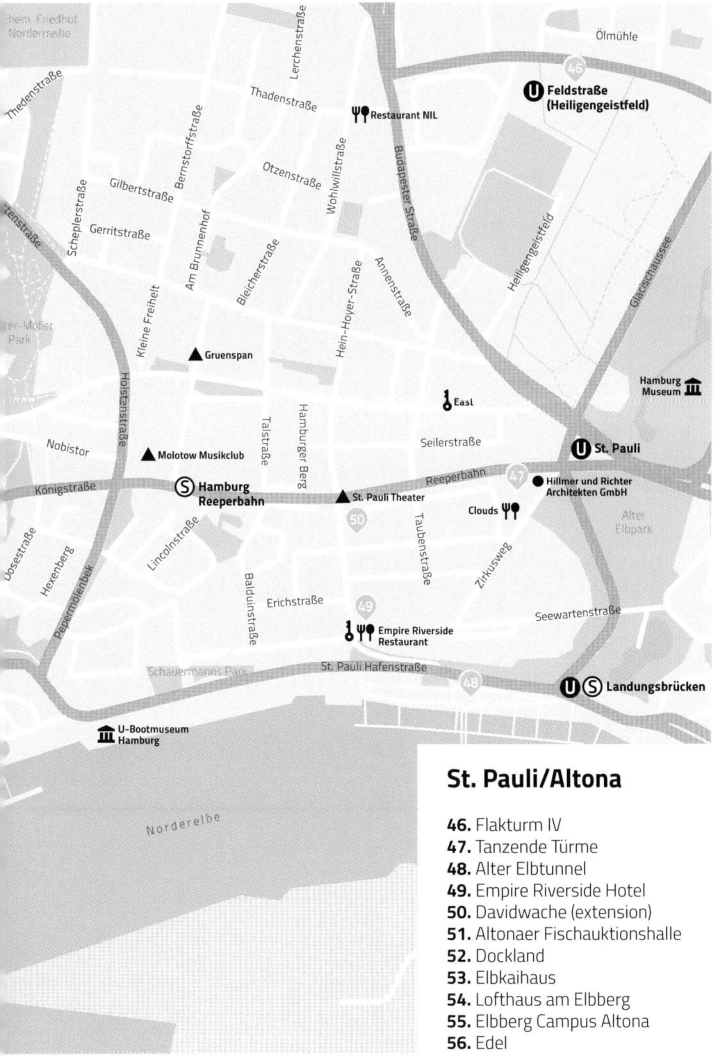

St. Pauli/Altona

46. Flakturm IV
47. Tanzende Türme
48. Alter Elbtunnel
49. Empire Riverside Hotel
50. Davidwache (extension)
51. Altonaer Fischauktionshalle
52. Dockland
53. Elbkaihaus
54. Lofthaus am Elbberg
55. Elbberg Campus Altona
56. Edel

46. Flakturm IV

Feldstraße 66
20359 Hamburg

limited access

U3
Feldstraße

3/602/X3
U Feldstraße

The reinforced cement bunker, in an area of the St. Pauli district called "Heiligengeistfeld" (Field of the Holy Spirit), was built in 1942 on a design by Friedrich Tamms, under the direction of Albert Speer, Inspector General for the Reich's capital. Another bunker in the same area was demolished in 1970.

Thousands of workers (both German and foreign) built the bunker to its massive proportions. Its base is 75×75 meters and the building is 39-meter high. Its outer wall is 3.5 meters thick and its ceiling, 5-meter thick. Built as a shelter for the people of Hamburg from enemy air attacks, the bunker had an 18,000-person capacity, though it held a great many more than that over the course of World War II.

In the post-war era, the bunker was used in response to severe housing shortages. It has recently been turned into a multi-media center run by companies in the media and entertainment industry.

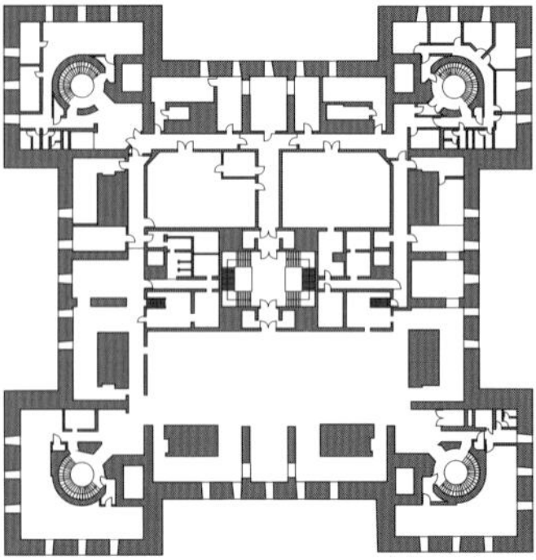

architect
Friedrich Tamms

type
bunker

construction
1942

47. Tanzende Türme

Reeperbahn 1
20359 Hamburg

external view only

U3
St. Pauli

17/36/37/112/601/
607/608/609/610/688
U St. Pauli

At the hinge point between the city center and the St. Pauli are the Tanzende Türme (Dancing Towers), buildings seemingly caught mid-dance. They are a joyous expression of movement conveying their power as solitary urban landmarks giving the area a new identity. The two towers (75- and 85-meter high) mark the entrance to St. Pauli and Altona as well as the harbor, serving as a gateway to Reeperbahn, Hamburg's world-famed entertainment district.

The project's takes off from the idea of building an expressive architectural structure in steel and glass to do justice to the location's heterogeneous nature and its meaning beyond the area. It marks the end point of a number of recent major architectural changes in the neighborhood.

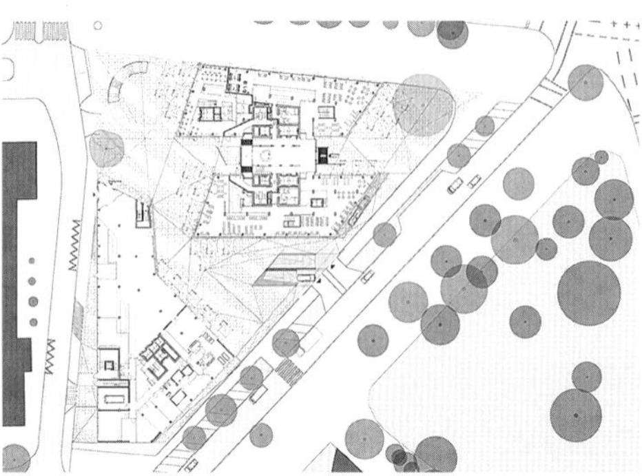

architects
Jens Bothe, Kai Richter,
Hadi Teherani

type
offices, hospitality

construction
2009-2011

48. Alter Elbtunnel

Bei den St. Pauli-
Landungsbrücken 7
20359 Hamburg

January - December
Mon - Sun / 05 am - 9 pm
December 31 / closed

+49 (0)40 428474742

U3
Landungsbrücken

S1/S2/S3
Landungsbrücken

111/608
U S Landungsbrücken
112
U S Jetties

62
Landungsbrücken
Brücke 3
61
Landungsbrücken
Brücke 2
72/73/75
Landungsbrücken
Brücke 1

The Alter Elbtunnel is 426-meter long and has two galleries. Built in the early twentieth century at 24 meters below ground level, the tunnel connects the two banks of the River Elbe, specifically Steinwerder Island with the St. Pauli district. The "alter" (old) in its name is because in 1975 another tunnel was opened nearby, cheerfully decked with majolica tiles depicting examples of marine life, served by four huge elevators and crossable by car, bike, or by foot.

The northern entrance features an entrance hall and dome made by Otto Wöhlecke and Ludwig Raabe.

architects
Philipp Holzmann, Otto Wöhlecke, Ludwig Raabe

type
tunnel

construction
1907-1911

49. Empire Riverside Hotel

Bernhard-Nocht-Straße 97
20359 Hamburg

external view only

+49 (0)40 311190
empire@hotel-hamburg.de
www.empire-riverside.de

U3
Landungsbrüken

S1/S2/S3
Landungsbrücken;
Reeperbahn

111
Bernhard-Nocht-Straße

The Empire Riverside Hotel and the Brauhaus, a retail and office building in the center of Hamburg above St. Pauli's docks in an area once home to the Bavaria brewery.

The project has three parts: a 328-room hotel made of a tower and an L-shaped base, the Brauhaus, and a square between the two. The three parts are a point of mediation between different urban contexts.

The hotel base and the Brauhaus make reference to the eaves of adjacent historic buildings. The hotel's soaring tower rises 21 floors, joining the Astra tower and the Michaeliskirche's bell tower to form a new "Hafenkrone", harbour crown. The hotel is divided into public and private areas. The public ones are in the building's base and on its 20th floor, which has a bar open to the public. As for its materials, the oak wood cladding panels and cement terrace contrast with the vibrant structure of the bronze and glass facade, made of prefabricated components.

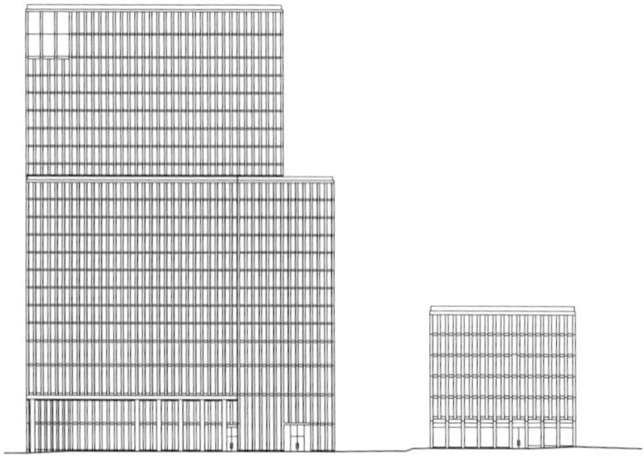

© David Chipperfield Architects

architects
David Chipperfield Architects

type
hotel, offices

construstion
2002-2007

50. Davidwache (extension)

Spielbudenplatz 31
20359 Hamburg

external view only

U3
St. Pauli

S1/S2/S3
Reeperbahn

36/37/111/601/607
608/609/641/688
Davidstraße

Davidwache was originally a house with a gabled roof designed by architect Fritz Schumacher in 1913. In 2005 a new box building with a flat roof was added to it, set where the two streets meet, and that corner was cut obliquely to enlarge the free space outside of it.

This extension is partially separated from the original building, but connected to it with a walkway, opening a dialogue with the older building while leaving it free and visible. The two buildings (currently a police headquarters) are fully clad in brick, which is darker and more austere in the new extension. Some floors in the connection area are finished with white plaster to help mark and foster the shift from old to new. The new building has solid parts and empty parts opened by glass bands that let us glimpse the interiors. It intentionally draws on the inspiration of the architect Schumacher, while declaring its contemporary architecture character.

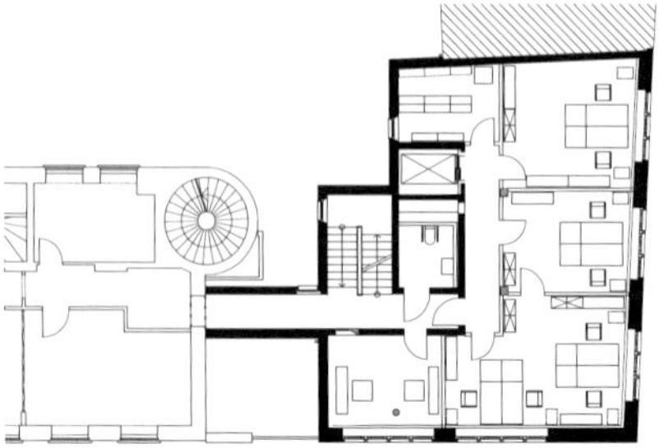

architects
Winking · Froh Architekten

type
offices

construction
2005

51. Altonaer Fischauktionshalle

Große Elbstraße 3
22767 Hamburg

April - September
Sun / 5.30 am - 12 am
October - March
Sun / 6 am - 12 am

+49 (0)40 570105200
info@fischauktionshalle.com
www.fischauktionshalle.com

S1/S2/S3
Königstraße;
Reeperbahn

111
Fischauktionshalle

61/62
Altona (Fischmarkt)

Altona's fish market, started in 1703, was located in a building built between 1895 and 1896 on the banks of the Elbe, later turned into a conference and events center by the Hamburg architect Günter Talkenberg and the center is still here today.

The iron, glass and stone building is oriented primarily horizontally and symmetrically. Its distinguishing feature is a large dome set at its center where the entrance is located. Its long, narrow interior is a completely free space, lit from the skylight that crosses the roof's ridge and from side openings. Its inner walls have balconies overlooking the central hall.

The building is one of Hamburg's most traditional, distinctive places, a representative of one of Germany's major important ports, making it well worth a visit on a Sunday morning to enjoy an excellent brunch.

architects
-

type
market

construction
1895-1896

52. Dockland

Van-der-Smissen-Straße 9
22767 Hamburg

external view only

www.dockland-hamburg.de

111
Kreuzfahrtterminal Altona

61/62
Dockland (Fischereihafen)

The Dockland Office Building is a gateway to Hamburg, located at the head of Edgar-Engelhard-Kai (Edgar Engelhard pier) between the Elbe and the harbor. The "bow" of the ship-shaped building juts more than 40 meters freely over the water, creating a dynamic addition to the "stern" of the nearby ferry terminal. The building is supported by a steel frame and has over 9,000 square meters of effective surface area.

The building's width makes the interiors very functional, accommodating conference rooms, archives, and service rooms in its central area. The large open areas with furnishings arranged freely throughout create a comfortable working atmosphere. The atmosphere is accentuated by large glass facades through which employees can enjoy a gorgeous view of the harbor landscape from their workstations. The building's roof terrace can be accessed by outside visitors through a public stairway at the back of the building. The terrace affords a gorgeous view and has a restaurant.

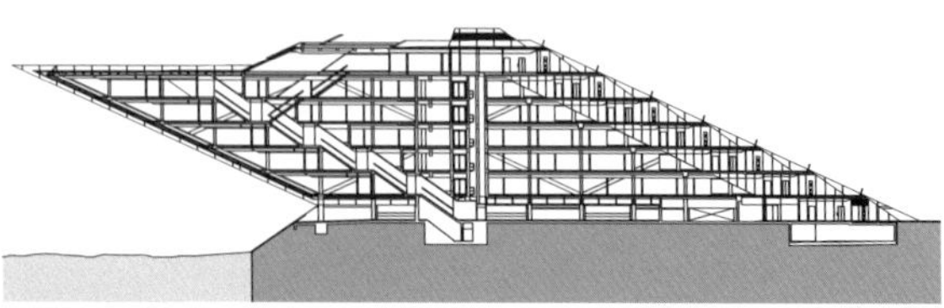

architects
Jens Bothe, Kai Richter,
Hadi Teherani

type
offices, restaurant

construction
2004-2006

53. Elbkaihaus

Große Elbstraße 145a-145f
22767 Hamburg

external view only

+49 (0)40 3801240
info@elbkaihaus.de
www.elbkaihaus.de

The Elbkaihaus was made from a renovation and partial reconstruction of a building built in 1965. Now, after having been renovated, the complex has 12,000 square meters for offices with an excellent view of the River Elbe, and is primarily home to new IT companies.

The 130-meter long building stretches along the Elbe's pier and is divided into five lots, each of which is accessible through a stairway or an elevator. The first and second floor of each steel and glass facade on the river are jutting and make the interiors open and particularly well lit. The structural design preserved much of the original reinforced concrete system and gave excellent flexibility in the spaces' internal division, organized in rentable units of different sizes.

Two recently restored cranes, each 30 meters high and weighing 71 tons, serve as emblems of the building complex and the area's original maritime history.

111
Kreuzfahrtterminal
Altona

61/62
Dockland
(Fischereihafen)

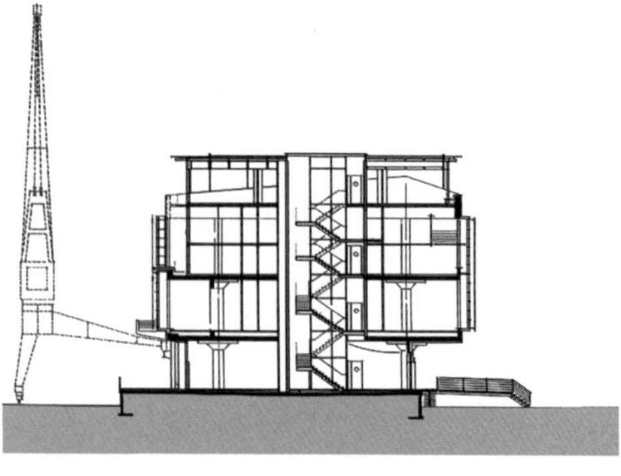

architects
gmp Architekten von Gerkan, Marg und Partner

type
offices

construction
1998-1999

54. Lofthaus am Elbberg

Elbberg 1
22767 Hamburg

external view only

The area around Hamburg's Elbberg features the contrast between the water of the River Elbe to the south, the steep tree-covered slope to the north, and the nearby fish warehouses and office buildings. The Lofthaus on Große Elbstraße makes references to these different worlds. For example, the southern glass facade has a fan-like configuration and suggests the lightness of water. Its counterpoint is the green copper facade, which is almost entirely closed and set on the uphill side of the building.

The building is on stilts, which protects it from waves, while accentuating its openness and lightness. The Lofthaus' highly distinctive appearance makes it a prominent part of the area's urban plan that seeks to convert this area of the River Elbe into a "string of pearls" of high-quality, flexible architectural works.

111
Kreuzfahrtterminal Altona
111/112
Elbberg

61/62
Dockland (Fischereihafen)

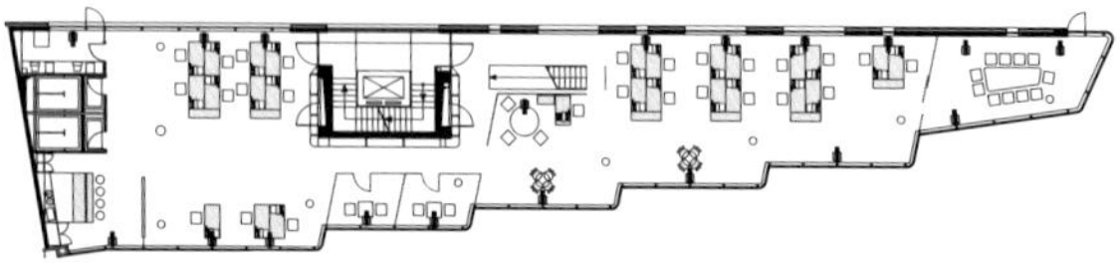

architects
Jens Bothe, Kai Richter,
Hadi Teherani

type
offices

construction
1996-1997

55. Elbberg Campus Altona

Große Elbstraße 264
22767 Hamburg

external view only

www.elbbergcampusaltona.de

The Elbberg Campus, on the Große Elbstraße combines work, housing, and leisure amidst warehouses, industrial sheds and green spaces. The complex's design is based on the site's existing lines. Buildings were built following the slope of a new park area and hold offices, homes, and lofts. New pedestrian paths, stairways and terraces connect the area to the Altona pier and to the harbor. The office building is also set within the public areas. The roof of its base volume serves as a large terrace, affording a spectacular view of the harbor.

Though private space and common space are distinctly marked in the complex, they are also harmoniously interwoven through its architectural and landscape design. The Elbberg Campus was inspired by the Treppenviertel (stairs neighborhood) Blankeneseis. It is another step forward in the restructuring plan for the Elbe's riverbank whose goal is to turn the area into a mixed-use zone.

111
Kreuzfahrtterminal
Altona
111/112
Elbberg

61/62
Dockland
(Fischereihafen)

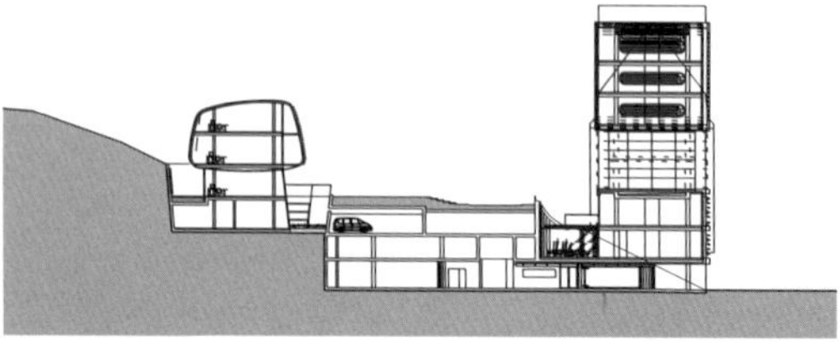

architects
Jens Bothe, Kai Richter,
Hadi Teherani

type
residential, offices

construction
2001-2003

56. Edel

Neumühlen 17
22763 Hamburg

limited access

112
Lawaetzhaus

61/62
Dockland
(Fischereihafen)

The new headquarters of the independent German recording company, Edel, is now housed in a five-story building on the banks of the Elba River to which it opens through a central courtyard. The design's volume is based on an urban plan to convert the old wharf by building several independent buildings on it.

On the first two floors, which are open to the public, the building has a restaurant, a cafe, a cafeteria, a showroom, and foyer, and a small auditorium. The other floors are for offices, face the Elbe and project from the base.

The first two floors' transparency reflects the primarily public nature of this part of the building, whose continuity with the adjacent areas is emphasized with large terraces. The building's variety of functions makes it and its adjacent free spaces still bustling after offices close in the evening.

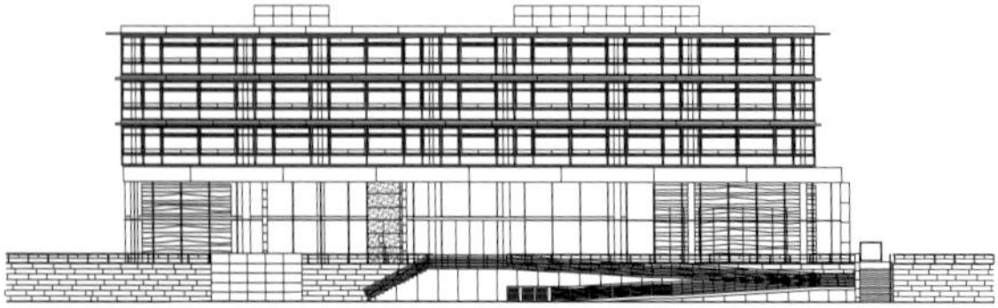

architects
Antonio Citterio Patricia Viel

type
commercial, restaurant, leisure

construction
1998-2002

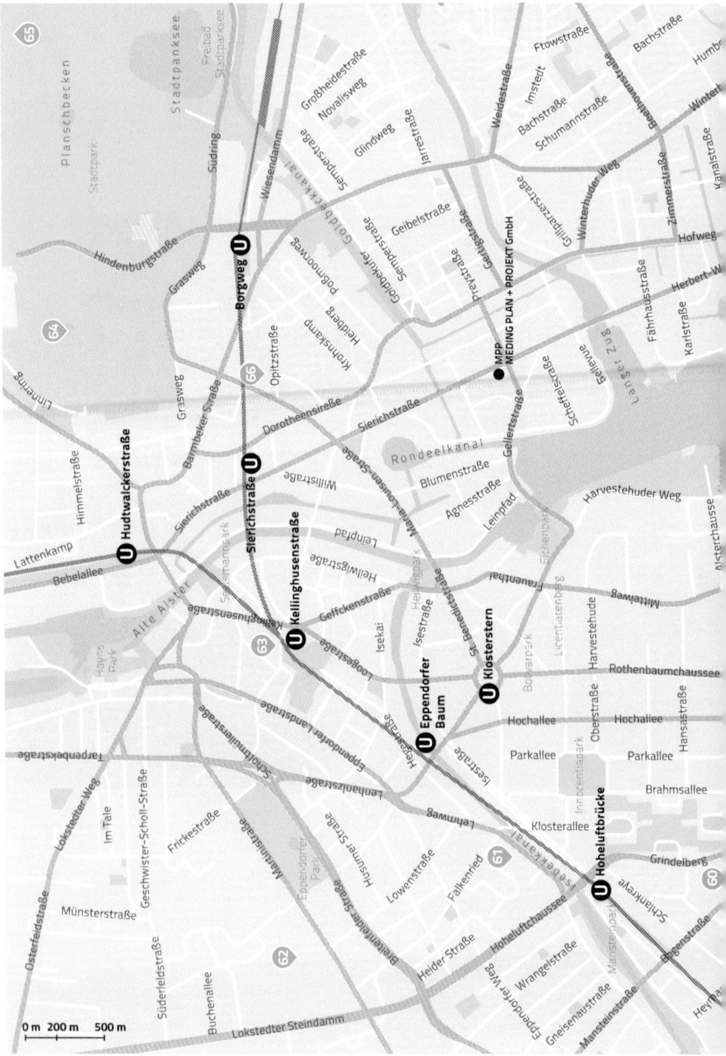

Planschbecken
Stadtpark
Stadtparksee
Freibad Stadtparksee
Hindenburgstraße
Südring
Grasweg
Borgweg
Wiesendamm
Großheidestraße
Novalisweg
Semperstraße
Glindweg
Jarrestraße
Goldbekkanal
Poßmoorweg
Heidberg
Krohnskamp
Opitzstraße
Geibelstraße
Semperstraße
Goldbekufer
Preystraße
Gertigstraße
Weidestraße
Imstedt
Bachstraße
Ftowstraße
Schumannstraße
Beethovenstraße
Grillparzerstraße
Winterhuder Weg
Zimmerstraße
Kanalstraße
Hofweg
Fährhausstraße
Herbert-W
Karlstraße
MPP
MEDING PLAN + PROJEKT GmbH
Scheffelstraße
Bellevue
Langer Zug
Linnering
Grasweg
Barmbeker Straße
Dorotheenstraße
Sierichstraße
Hudtwalckerstraße
Himmelstraße
Sierichstraße
Willistraße
Rondeelkanal
Blumenstraße
Agnesstraße
Leinpfad
Gellertstraße
Harvestehuder Weg
Maria-Louisen-Straße
Lattenkamp
Bebelallee
Kellinghusenstraße
Leinpfad
Heilwigstraße
Seelemannpark
Alte Alster
Hayns Park
Kellinghusenstraße
Geffckenstraße
Heilwigpark
Isekai
Isestraße
St. Benediktstraße
Klosterstern
Frauenthal
Eichenpark
Licentiatenberg
Harvestehude
Mittelweg
Alsterchaussee
Bolivarpark
Rothenbaumchaussee
Loogestraße
Eppendorfer Baum
Hochallee
Oberstraße
Hansastraße
Eppendorfer Landstraße
Hegestraße
Schottmüllerstraße
Tarpenbekstraße
Isestraße
Parkallee
Innocentiapark
Brahmsallee
Lehnhalzstraße
Lehmweg
Klosterallee
Isebekkanal
Hoheluftbrücke
Grindelberg
Lokstedter Weg
Im Tale
Geschwister-Scholl-Straße
Frickestraße
Martinistraße
Eppendorfer Park
Husumer Straße
Lowenstraße
Falkenried
Schlankreye
Osterfeldstraße
Münsterstraße
Süderfeldstraße
Buchenallee
Breitenfelder Straße
Heider Straße
Hoheluftchaussee
Eppendorfer Weg
Wrangelstraße
Gneisenaustraße
Mansteinstraße
Mansteinpark
Bogenstraße
Lokstedter Steindamm
0 m 200 m 500 m
60
61
62
63
64
65
66

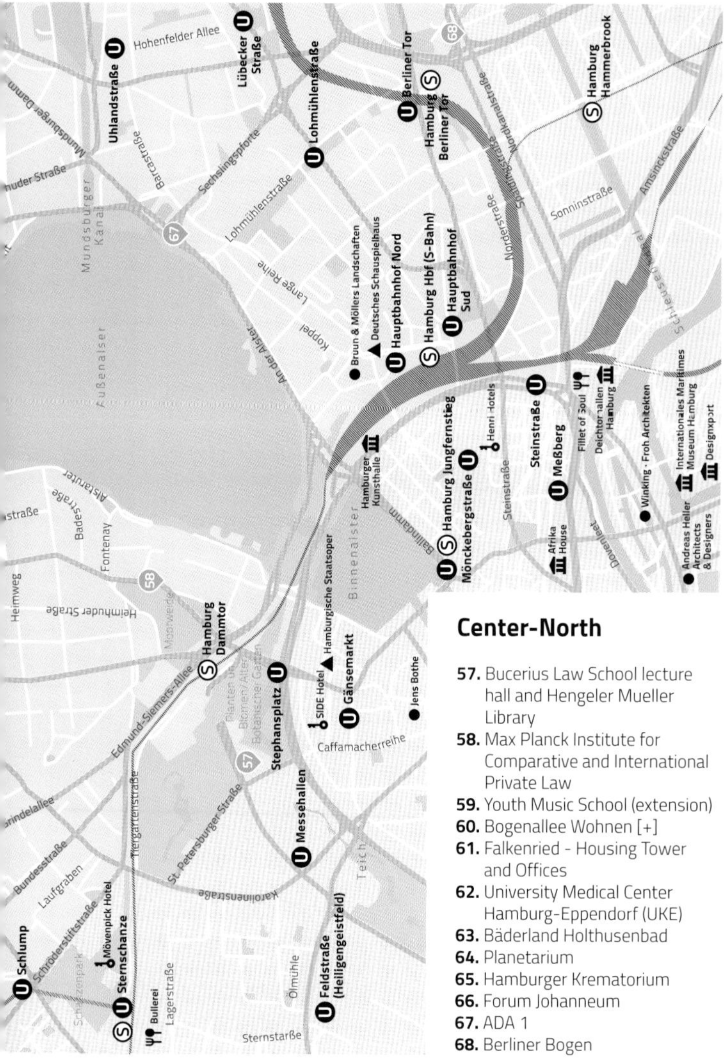

Center-North

57. Bucerius Law School lecture hall and Hengeler Mueller Library
58. Max Planck Institute for Comparative and International Private Law
59. Youth Music School (extension)
60. Bogenallee Wohnen [+]
61. Falkenried - Housing Tower and Offices
62. University Medical Center Hamburg-Eppendorf (UKE)
63. Bäderland Holthusenbad
64. Planetarium
65. Hamburger Krematorium
66. Forum Johanneum
67. ADA 1
68. Berliner Bogen

57. Bucerius Law School lecture hall and Hengeler Mueller Library

Jungiusstraße 6
20355 Hamburg

access by appointment

+49 (0)40 30706127
klaus.weber@law-school.de
www.law-school.de

U1
Stephansplatz
U2
Messehallen

A1/IC/ICE/EC/IC/N/ RB61/RE
Hamburg Dammtor

35
Hamburg Messe (Eingang Ost)

The expansion of the Bucerius Law School was done in phases and entailed building a new lecture hall-auditorium and a large library. The lecture hall building was the first to be opened and evokes the historical concept of a Tempietto garden. The large structure is a Reuleaux triangle made of three circular arches and is clad with glass panels. The area between the auditorium structure and the glazed facade serves as an insulating air gap protecting against the elements.

The library building was conceived as a symbolic version of the winter gardens common in the area. On the building's top floors is the large library that can easily accommodate about 560 people. On the ground floor are a conference room, seating several hundred, and a new cafeteria/coffee shop. The facade clearly evokes the building's function on the campus with colored glass panels inspired by the sight of books on shelves.

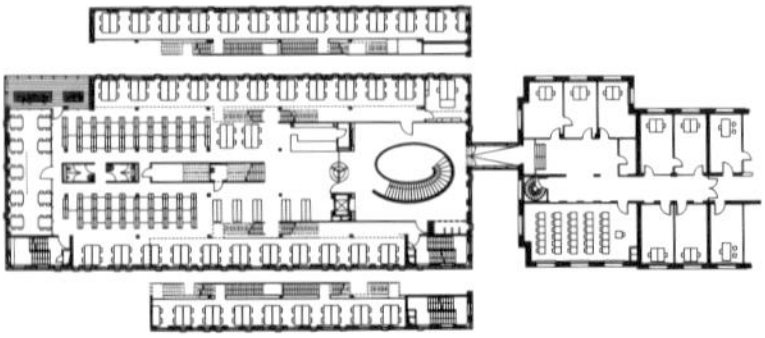

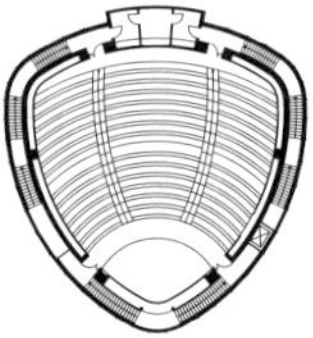

architects	type	construction
MPP Meding Plan + Projekt	school, library, auditorium	2003-2007

58. Max Planck Institute for Comparative and International Private Law

Mittelweg 187
20148 Hamburg

external view only

+49 (0)40 419000
www.mpipriv.de

The building consists of three structures surrounding a courtyard, joining an existing complex. The new extension creates a new entrance for the entire complex and gives the institute 3,600 square meters of new floor area and 2,000 square meters of underground space for archives.

The public facilities are on the ground floor, near the entrance. The library connects the ground floor and the basement. The first and second floor are primarily for offices and apartments (which have a separate entrance). The third floor is for conferences.

The new building fits in the complex by using copper, the same material on the facade cladding of the original buildings.

A1/IC/ICE/EC/IC/N/ RB61/RE
Hamburg Dammtor

19/605
Bf. Dammtor;
Fontenay

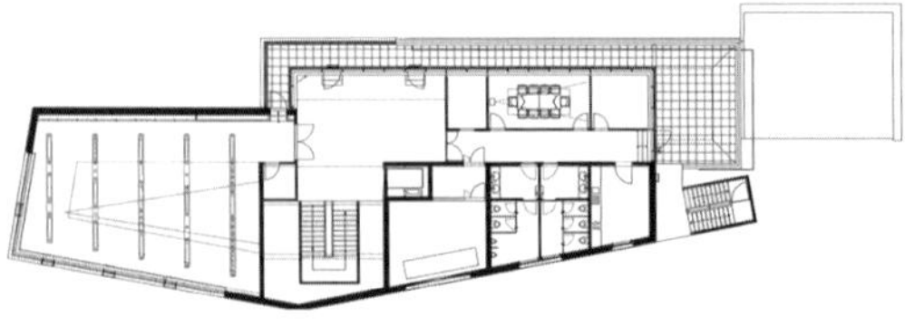

architects
bof architekten

type
research institute

construction
2005-2006

59. Youth Music School (extension)

Mittelweg 42
20148 Hamburg

access by appointment

+49 (0)40 428014141
info-jms@bsb.hamburg.de

U1
Hallerstraße

19/605
Alsterchaussee

The construction of the new music school, completed in 2000, planned from the start for an expansion, which was completed ten years later. The expansion between the old and new music schools is in a position to create a corridor between the two complexes.

It forges a powerful dialogue with the garden and original school. The new auditorium on the first floor directly connects to the classrooms, leaving a large multi-purpose space on the ground floor below it where the main foyer is located. The new auditorium almost completely covers the lot between the school's L-shaped buildings on the area's northern and western edges.

The materials used evoke those already in the surroundings, such as the colors of the brick church and school buildings which are expanded to five colors for the auditorium's curved walls clad in ceramic and suggest sound waves. The shelter set above the entrance is zinc, also used for the ramp's structure.

architects
Benedetta Tagliabue –
Miralles Tagliabue EMBT

type
school

construction
2010-2011

60. Bogenallee Wohnen [+]

Bogenallee 10-12
20144 Hamburg

external view only

U1
Hoheluftbrücke

5/604
Bezirksamt Eimsbüttel
181
Bogenstraße

Located in the Harvestehude district, by the Grindelallee area and Rotherbaum and Eimsbüttel districts, the Bogenalle apartment building was made from a conversion of an office complex built around 1970.

The property includes 15 apartments of varying types, on four floors, joined by an underground level with 23 parking spots accessed by a platform lift.

The apartments are all based on high quality. Those on the ground floor have terraces facing the courtyard. On the upper floor they have large balconies and "flex boxes", large, adaptable living spaces projecting outwards. These elements serve as genuine extensions of the kitchen spaces, bedrooms, or bathrooms and give the facade on the Bogenalle their character. This facade and the longitudinal one are entirely clad by horizontally placed wood slats.

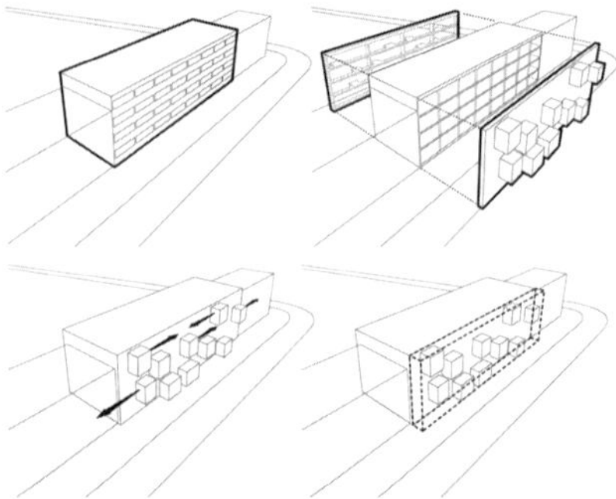

architects
Blauraum Architekten

type
residential

construction
2005

61. Falkenried - Housing Tower and Offices

Straßenbahnring 9
20251 Hamburg

external view only

U3
Hoheluftbrücke

The office and residential complex is in a former industrial district originally primarily for bus and tram depots and garages. The new design powerfully evokes Hamburg's expressionist architecture through two buildings whose site plans are highly original. The long, horizontally zigzagging building culminates in a high tower at one end. The second building, separated from the public square by the tower, follows a broken line.

The entire complex is unified by the regular organization of the glazed windows that open on its surface, clad entirely in dark brick, leaving room for irregular elements that jut from the surface line and project outwards.

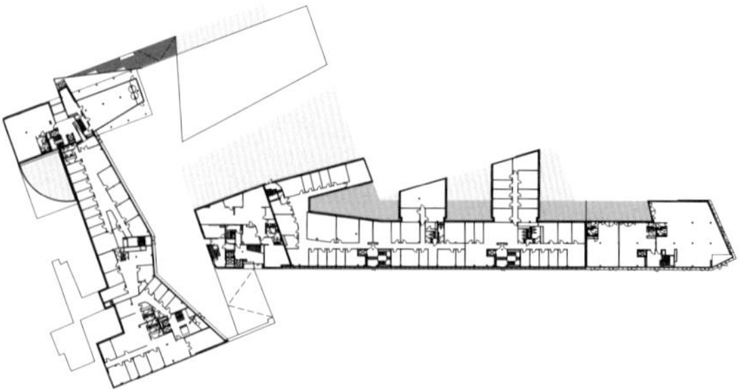

architects
BOLLES+WILSON

type
residential, offices

construction
2002-2004

62. University Medical Center Hamburg-Eppendorf (UKE)

Martinistraße 52
20251 Hamburg

open to public

+49 (0)40 74100
info@uke.de
www.uke.de

U3
Eppendorfer Baum

20/25/600
Eppendorfer Park (UKE);
UK Eppendorf

The building is made up of a pavilion structure organized on a hinged system, creating a balance between the historic "hospital in the park" arrangement and the need to consolidate its functions.

As the center of the complex, the second floor was designed like a boulevard to stroll along with a library, coffee shop, restaurant, shops, hairdresser, Internet points, and a bank. The areas where patients are examined and treated are placed beneath the boulevard, on the ground floor path and on the first floor, where they are not disturbed by passing visitors. The functional areas are streamlined to shorten the routees for patients and staff; and the design strives to create an attractive, inviting environment. The lighting concept and the spaces' clear arrangement create a sense of emotional security and an open, relaxed atmosphere.

The facade is adorned by a complex structure of vertical features. A seemingly random series of stonework walls, glass panels and sunbreakers conceal the function of the rooms behind the facade.

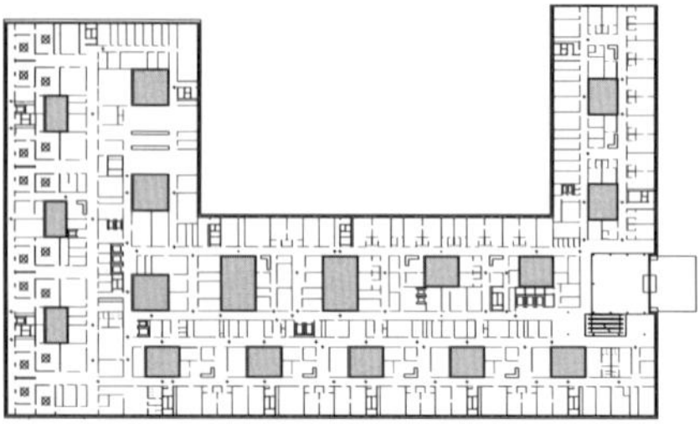

architects
Nickl & Partner
Architekten AG

type
university, hospital

construction
2004-2009

63. Bäderland Holthusenbad

Goernestraße 21
20249 Hamburg

September - April
Mon - Sun / 9 am - 11 pm
May - August
Mon - Sun / 9 am - 10 pm

+49 (0)40 188890
www.baederland.de/bad/holthusenbad.php

U1/U3
Kellinghusenstraße

25/26
U Kellinghusenstraße

Built on the design of the architect Fritz Schumacher, the building was inaugurated in 1914 as a place for the public to bathe as well as an oasis of health. Within its grand dimensions it originally held two swimming pools, one for men and one for women, set by the two large side windows which open to the light the two vaulted rooms perpendicular to the facade. After closing during World War II, it was reopened in 1937 and mixed-gender bathing was introduced.

The building, which fits with Hamburg's architectural tradition of exposed brickwork, was restored and changed in its use many times over the years. Particularly the central wing, which covers three floors, has seen the addition of a library, municipal offices, and medical clinics. Currently the building houses a state-of-the-art wellness center, including indoor and outdoor swimming pools and spas.

architect
Fritz Schumacher

type
swimming pool, spa

construction
1913-1914

64. Planetarium

Linnering 1
22299 Hamburg

January - December
Mon - Tue / 9 am - 5 pm
Wed - Thu / 9 am - 9 pm
Fri / 9 am - 10 pm
Sat / 12 am - 10 pm
Sun / 10 am - 8 pm

+49 (0)40 428865210
info@planetarium-hamburg.de
www.planetarium-hamburg.de

U1
Hudtwalckerstraße;
Lattenkamp
U3
Borgweg

179
Stadtpark (Planetarium)
20/26
Ohlsdorfer Straße
(Planetarium)

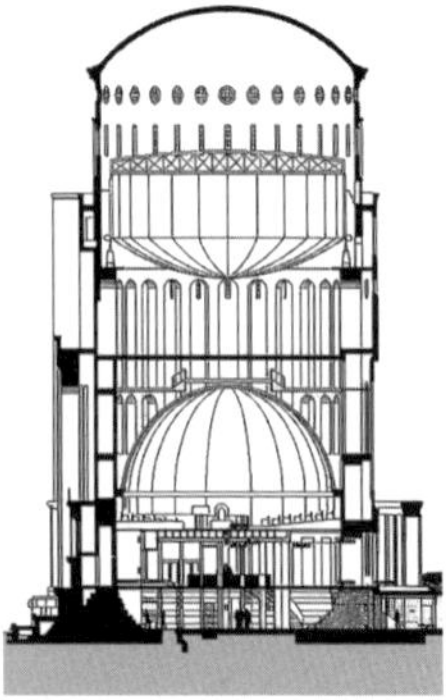

The Planetarium is in a stonework building originally a water tower. The project was built under the supervision of the architect Fritz Schumacher in Stadtpark and was opened to the public in 1930 after Hamburg's city government decided to buy a Zeiss planetarium (Model II, now the Universarium Mk.9). Today's technology, controlled by about 30 computers and using fiberglass cables, gives us an almost flawless vision of "the world's most beautiful sky" projected on a dome with a diameter of about 21 meters. The tower is an architectural landmark for Hamburg and can also be climbed, its roof terrace making an impressive viewpoint.

architect
Fritz Schumacher
(director of works)

type
planetarium

construction
1912-1917

65. Hamburger Krematorium

Talstraße
22337 Hamburg

access by appointment

Mon - Thu / 9.30 am - 3 pm

+49 (0)40 59388702
www.krematorium-hamburg.de

U1
Klein Borstel

S1/S11
Ohlsdorf

170
Friedhof Ohlsdorf (Bestattungsforum)
172
Im Grünen Grunde
172/174/274/392
U S Ohlsdorf (Im Grünen Grunde)

The dark clinker brick building was designed by architect Fritz Schumacher to replace the original crematorium from 1891. It is in the Ohlsdorf cemetery area and includes several structures placed side by side to form a symmetrical system whose line is oriented to the organization of the surrounding site.

A large memorial hall is in the center of the complex, now named "Fritz Schumacher Hall". It has a gable roof with a particularly pronounced pitch supported by arches that define the character of the interior along with stained glass windows. The operational areas are in the basement rooms. This was one of Schumacher's last works; he took particular care in designing and choosing its techniques and materials, including terracotta, stained glass, mosaics, and metal, symbolically suggesting fire. For each technique, he called on expert artists and craftsmen, including Richard Kuöhl for the terracotta, used for the bas-reliefs on the external facades, and the Hungarian artist Ervin Bossányi for the window decorations, and Heinrich Jungebloedt for the mosaics.

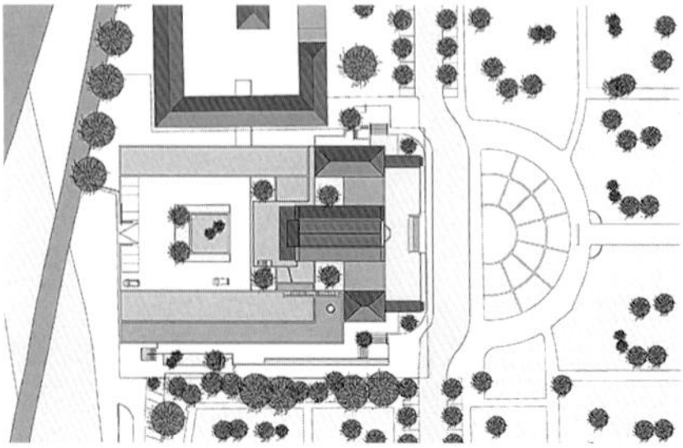

architect
Fritz Schumacher

type
crematorium

construction
1928-1932

66. Forum Johanneum

Maria-Louisen-Straße 114
22301 Hamburg

access by appointment

+49 (0)40 4288270
www.johanneum-hamburg.de

U3
Sierichstraße

19/25/606
U Sierichstraße
600
Maria-Louisen-Straße (Nord)

The Forum is an expansion of Gelehrtenschule des Johanneums, one of Germany's oldest gymnasium schools, founded in 1529 and built between 1912 and 1914 on Fritz Schumacher's design. The recent expansion involved the construction of a new building, the result of a joint project by the school's Director, the Department of Culture of the City of Hamburg and Andreas Heller's architectural firm.

Though it dialogues with the original building, the new building (which holds spaces for teaching art, music and theater, as well as a gym and school cafeteria) is completely independent, both in its location and its architectural composition. The new design is a composition of a square and a complex of structures forming a C enclosed in a square site plan. Great care was taken in choosing and installing materials with the goal of forging a relationship with the historic brick building through a contemporary architectural vocabulary.

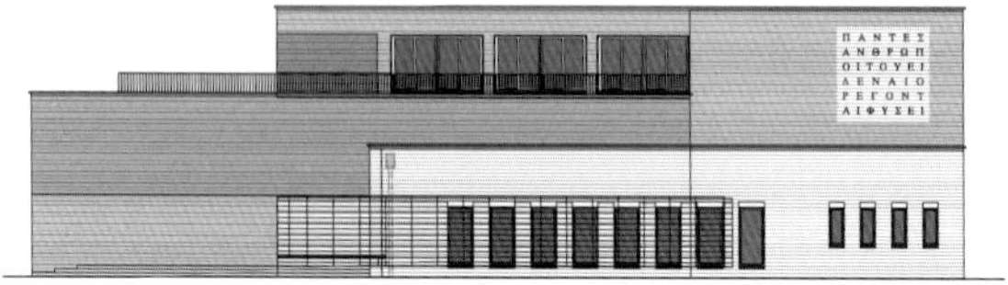

architects
Andreas Heller
Architects & Designers

type
school

construction
2005-2007

67. ADA 1

An der Alster 1
20099 Hamburg

external view only

The building is set at the intersection of Hamburg's city center and its natural landscape of water and plant life. The facade features floating "eyes" of different widths forming horizontal bands, celebrating the view of its particular setting facing a public park. The facade's "eyes" are echoed in the platforms with rounded corners placed throughout the park.

Allowing for a variety of functional organizations there are large spans and office interiors that can be arranged in diverse layouts.

U1
Lohmühlenstraße

6/17/37/607
AK St. Georg

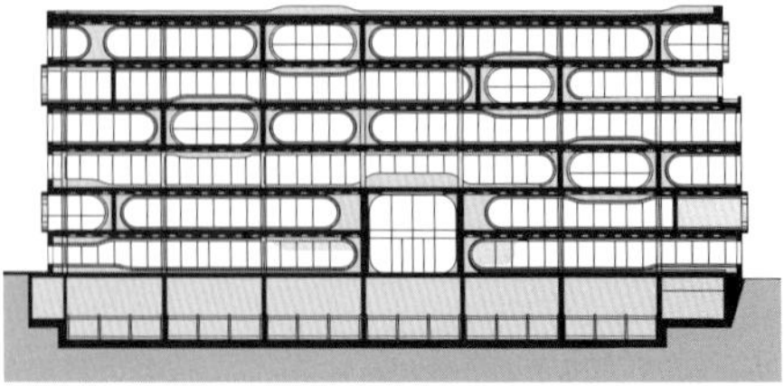

architects
Jürgen Mayer H. und Partner, Architekten

type
offices

construction
2005-2007

68. Berliner Bogen

Anckelmannsplatz
20537 Hamburg

external view only

U2/U3/U4
Berliner Tor

S1/S2/S11/S21/S31
Berliner Tor

154/160/261/ S21-SEV
U S Berliner Tor (Bürgerweide)
160
Normannenweg

The Berliner Bogen (Arch of Berlin) office building on Hamburg's Anckelmannsplatz looks as if it is suspended over the water. The glass building stretches 140 meters above the end section of a several-kilometer long expansion dock, creating valuable land area for development within the city. Steel parabolic arches rest on either side of the river, rising up to 36 meters above the canal. The building was designed as a "house in a house". A glass envelope encloses a comb-like form whose 32,000 square meters make room for 1,200 workstations. The structure is visually impressive and offers excellent energy savings. The buffer zones between the core and the skin of the structure let the offices be naturally ventilated and helps cut heating costs in half. The six indoor window gardens are rest spaces for employees and a space for exhibitions and parties.

The building's exceptional appearance, well-considered spatial organization and modern energy concept make it a dynamic gateway joining the water and city.

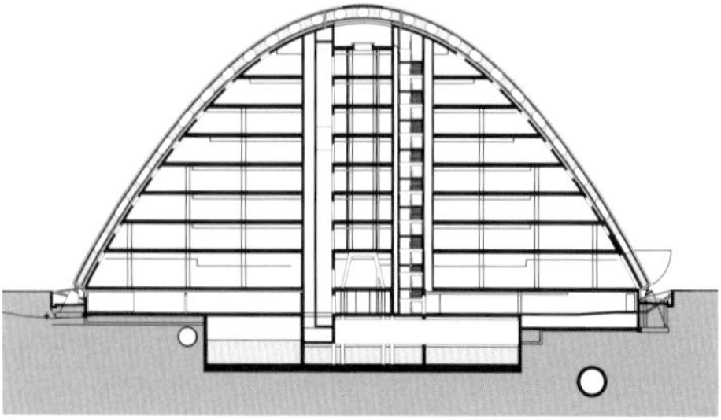

© Matteo Mostardini

architects
Jens Bothe, Kai Richter,
Hadi Teherani

type
offices

construction
1998-2001

Veddeler Damm
Niedernfelder Ufer
Spreehafen
Harburger Chaussee
Harburger Chaussee
Hafenrandstraße
Stenzelring
Schlenzigstraße
Vogelhüttendeich
Ernst-August-Kanal
Schiffsgraben
Fährstraße
Fährstraße
Industriestraße
Manesallee
Veringstraße
Zeidlerstraße
Weimarer Straße
Georg-Wilhelm-Straße
Rubbertstraße
Neuhöfer Straße
72
71
WilhelmsRock
Zeidlerstraße
Aßmannkanal
Jaffe-Davids-Kanal
Veringkanal
Veringstraße
Rotenhäuser Damm
Jaffestraße
Rotenhäuser Straße
Bei der Wollkämmerei
Bonifatiusstraße
Dratelnstraße
Rotenhäuser End
Korallusstraße
Georg-Wilhelm-Straße
Am Bahngraben
Schlengendeich
Mengestraße
Dratelnstraße
Wittestraße
79
80
Wilhelmsburg
Wilhelmsburger Rathauspark
78
77
76
Am Inselpark
75
74
Krieterstr
Kurdamm
73
0 m
200 m
500 m

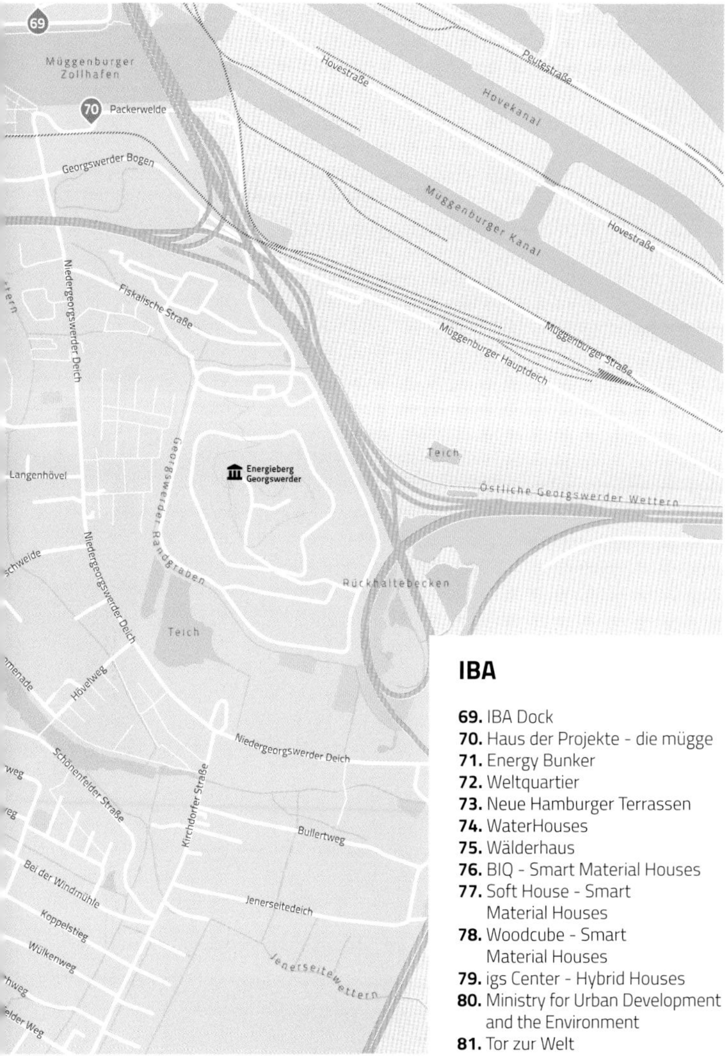

IBA

69. IBA Dock
70. Haus der Projekte - die mügge
71. Energy Bunker
72. Weltquartier
73. Neue Hamburger Terrassen
74. WaterHouses
75. Wälderhaus
76. BIQ - Smart Material Houses
77. Soft House - Smart Material Houses
78. Woodcube - Smart Material Houses
79. igs Center - Hybrid Houses
80. Ministry for Urban Development and the Environment
81. Tor zur Welt

69. IBA Dock

Am Zollhafen 12
20539 Hamburg

open to the public

www.iba-hamburg.de

S3/S31
Veddel (BallinStadt)

34/154/254/354/640
Wilhelmsburger Platz

The IBA Dock was built near the port of Müggenburg at the entrance to the IBA area. In February 2010, it became IBA Hamburg GmbH's official headquarters.

The rectangular building is a 50×26 meter floating platform, built through the assembly of steel modules, which can be partly disassembled should the building be moved.

Like all of the area's projects, the IBA Dock contributes to developing new technological systems for sustainable building. In addition to insulating external walls, it uses Sun and water to generate the energy needed for the heat pump that heats it. The project was intelligently designed to handle floods. The base platform adopts to the natural variations in water level, raising and lowering as much as 3.5 meters.

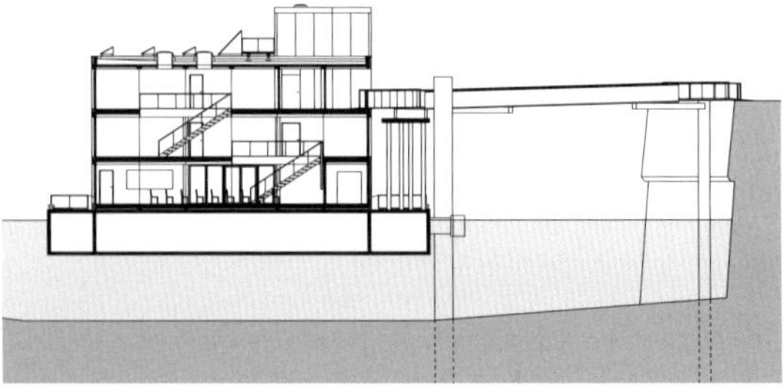

© IBA Hamburg / Han Slavik

architects	**type**	**construction**
Han Slawik Architekt	info center, cafe	2009-2010

70. Haus der Projekte - die mügge

Packersweide 7
20539 Hamburg

external view only

www.diemuegge.de

S3/S31
Veddel (BallinStadt)

The building was designed as a training center for unemployed youth with a focus on boat building. It is located by the Müggenburg port at the northern end of the IBA facing the IBA Dock. The building came out of a competition put on by IBA Hamburg GmbH jointly with "Get the Kick e.V." In the archetypical shape of a house, the building's energy supply is from a self-powering hydrogen and oxygen system. It is organized as a workshop-garage from which boats can be moved by a crane from the interior workshop to the covered outdoor area on the water.

Inside there are also offices and common areas for recreation as well as a kitchen. The spaces are on several levels connected by an outdoor steel stairway. The entire building is clad externally with corrugated iron sheets, optimally insulating the rooms in combination with an internal wooden frame.

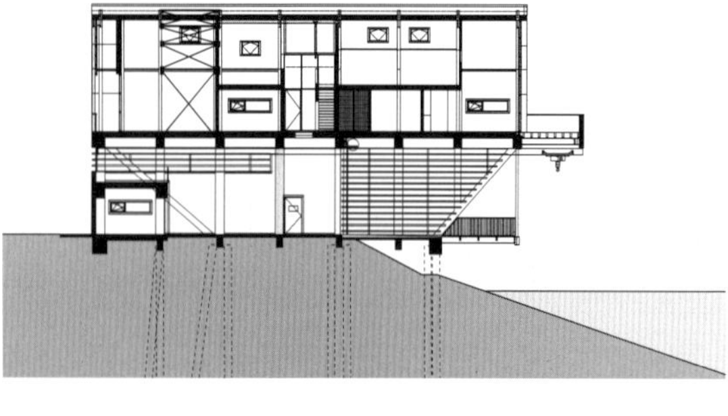

architects
Studio NL-D

type
offices, school

construction
2010-2012

71. Energy Bunker

Neuhöfer Straße 7
21107 Hamburg

Mon - Thu / closed
Fri / 12 am - 6 pm
Sat - Sun / 10 am - 6 pm

This bunker in the Wilhelmsburg district has been turned into the largest solar power plant in Europe. Designed by architect Friedrich Tamms in 1943, the bunker was devastated by the British army in 1947 and was left virtually unused for over sixty years. Today the building has been completely renovated and put at the service of the environment, becoming a plant powered by renewable energy sources (solar, biogas, wood chips, as well as heat from waste of a nearby industrial plant). It can heat the Reiherstieg district and part of Hamburg, simultaneously creating electricity and heat.

The history of the bunker and the former residents of the Reiherstieg's district are featured in an exhibition organized inside and around the building. The Vju Café and its terrace, set 30 meters up, afford a unique view of the city and its harbor.

34/151/152/252/640
Neuhöfer Straße (Ost)

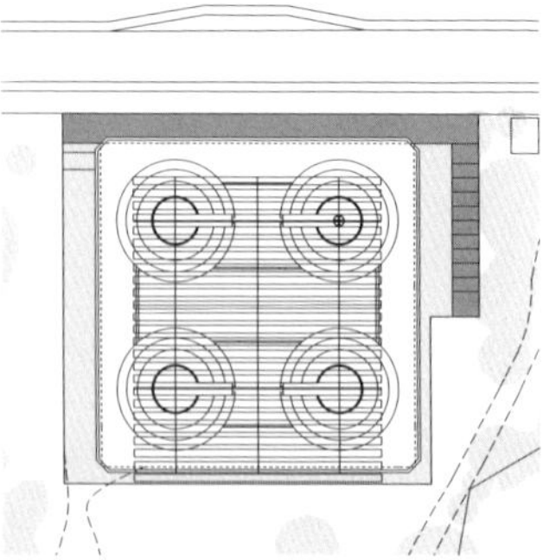

© IBA Hamburg / HHS Planer + Architekten AG

architects	**type**	**construction**
HHS Planer + Architekten AG	museum, cafe	2010-2013

72. Weltquartier

Weimarer Straße, Neuhöfer Straße, Veringstraße
21107 Hamburg

external view only

151/152/252/13/156
Veringstraße (Mitte)

The Weltquartier (Quarter of Nations) is one of the projects included in the IBA Hamburg 2013 initiative, based on the key theme "Cosmopolis". The experimental projects are primarily aimed at demonstrating potential cooperation schemes in urban environments, and are proposed as possible models for intercultural living.

The purpose of this operation was to answer the housing needs of a multi-ethnic population of over 30 different nationalities, and, within the concept, to try to integrate the different customs and lifestyles of the inhabitants through a participatory process executed in several stages.

The project adopted two complementary approaches. On one hand, it focused on the redevelopment of the existing neighborhood composed of port workers' housing: low, red-brick constructions with gabled roofs, built in the 1930s. At the same time, the project constructed new housing complexes, designed to blend harmoniously with the pre-existing buildings, using the same materials, classification, and architectural style.

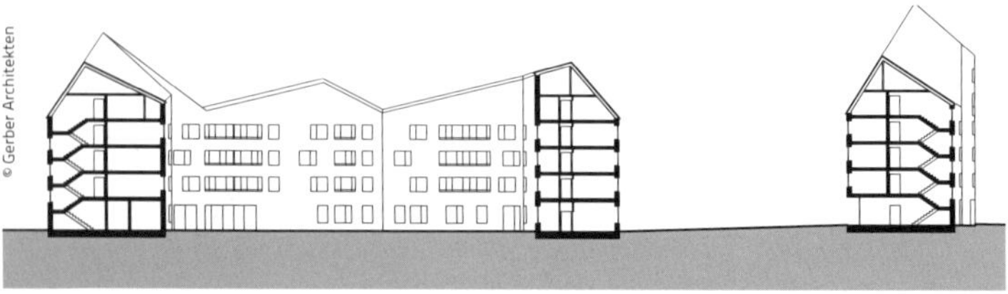

architects
Gerber Architekten

type
residential

construction
2012-2014

73. Neue Hamburger Terrassen

Schlöperstieg
21107 Hamburg

external view only

www.neue-hamburger-terrassen.de

S3/S31
Wilhelmsburg

The residential complex includes 33 apartments joined in four adjacent units. The design by the French firm LAN was developed in a participatory project with its future inhabitants part of a 'Baugruppe'. It draws on Hamburg's architectural heritage, evoking workers' row houses in a contemporary style to create townhouses and multi-floor units.

From reflection on the individual home, the car, the definition and prioritization of public and collective spaces, as well as environmental quality, the project aims at producing a new, sustainable urban model, based on a vernacular typology.

The U-shaped volumes of the housing increase the intimacy of the yards and accentuate the connection with the park located to the east. Each housing block has 6-10 residences, of two kinds: "row-house" and "multi-level" units. The variations in the constructions, the programs, surfaces, and the material finishings reveal the potential of the typology that was created, and they bear witness to its wealth. The neighborhood has remained very consistent in terms of its architectural vocabulary, and yet, each residence is unique.

architects
LAN architecture,
Christoph Konerding Architekt
(construction phase)

type
residential

construction
2011-2013

74. WaterHouses

Am Inselpark 10-18 (equal)
21109 Hamburg

external view only

www.waterhouses.de

S3/S31
Wilhelmsburg

**13/34/151/152/154
156/252/640**
Inselpark

In no other German city is water as essential a part of the city identity as it is in Hamburg. Nonetheless, until recently, building on the water was limited to a few cases, now the IBA area includes a residential complex built completely on water.

The WaterHouses complex includes four buildings and a tower. It is built on pillars whose bases are sunk into a water basin of about 4,000 square meters. The four buildings are on three stacked levels corresponding to the three floors of each apartment (called Triplexes); the tower has nine floors. All the apartments have balconies or terraces with views, in a close relationship with the water, including through large glazed panels.

The heat for the residents' daily use is provided by renewable energy sources, including the basin's water, which fuels a geothermal heat pump. There are also technological systems, such as solar components that make up the external cladding.

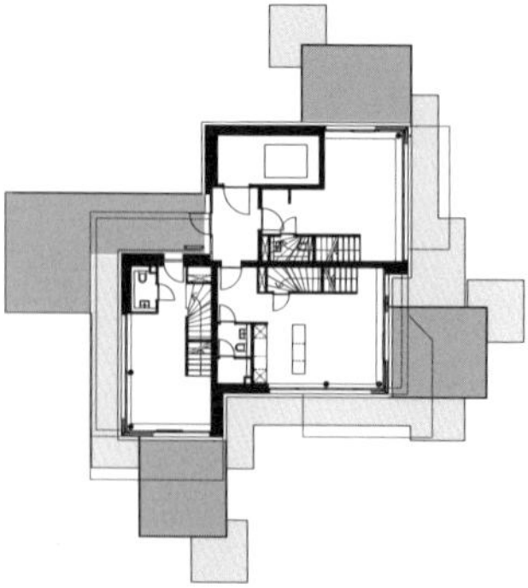

architects
Schenk + Waiblinger
Architekten

type
residential

construction
2011-2013

75. Wälderhaus

Am Inselpark 19
21109 Hamburg

open to the public

+49 (0)40 3021560
info@waelderhaus.de
www.waelderhaus.de

S3/S31
Wilhelmsburg

13/34/151/152/154
156/252/640
Inselpark

The Wälderhaus (The Forest House) is a multi-purpose five-storey building that includes a space for exhibitions and conferences on forest and sustainability-related themes, as well as a restaurant, the Wilhelms im Wälderhaus, and a three-star hotel, the Raphael Hotel Wälderhaus, with 82 rooms on the three upper floors.

The variety of functions is underscored by different materials. The first two floors are reinforced concrete. The three hotel floors are solid spruce wood with European certification. A green roof was created as a habitat suitable to certain species of trees and bushes and small animals, as well as to improve the city's microclimate. The shape of the building is inspired by the stump of a tree.

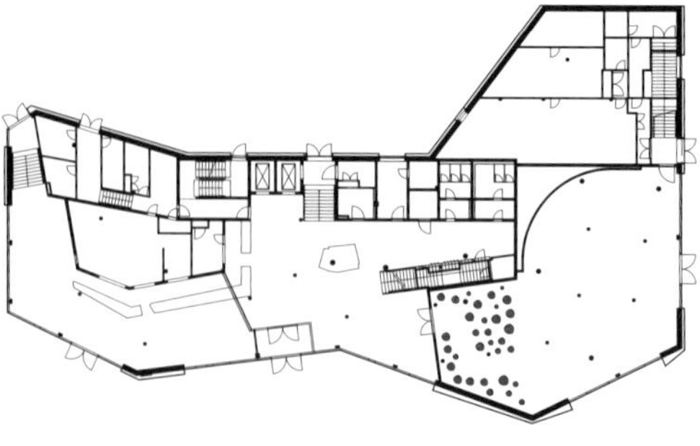

architects
Andreas Heller
Architects & Designers

type
offices, museum,
restaurant, hotel

construction
2010-2012

76. BIQ - Smart Material Houses

Am Inselpark 17
21109 Hamburg

external view only

www.biq-wilhelmsburg.de

Natural, efficient and absolutely unique, the BIQ residential building is the first in the world to have a bio-reactive facade, designed to state-of-the-art precepts of environmental sustainability, demonstrating the potential of new building technologies.

The two southern facades with the greatest Sun exposure have a second glass shell outside of the facade cladding. The glass facade holds micro-algae fed by sunlight, liquid nutrients, and carbon dioxide. Once the micro-algae have grown, they are transferred to a technical room where they are harvested for biogas and other energy substances. The algae also help control the lighting and shading of the interiors.

The building's compositional design also lets residents use the interior spaces, which can be organized very flexibly, plus large balconies opening on the green space around the building.

S3/S31
Wilhelmsburg

13/34/151/152/154
156/252/640
Inselpark

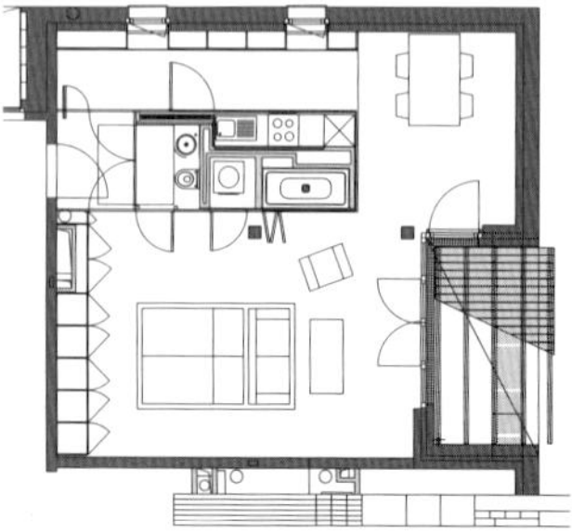

© IBA Hamburg / Splitterwerk

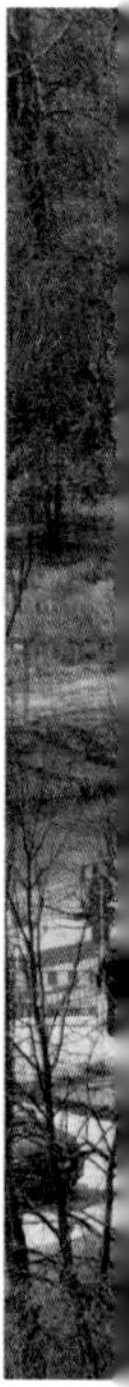

architects
Splitterwerk, Arup, B+G Ingenieure, Immosolar

type
residential

construction
2011-2013

77. Soft House - Smart Material Houses

Am Inselpark 5
21109 Hamburg

external view only

www.iba-hamburg.de

The Soft House is a residential building of four family units, which each cover three floors and have a private garden.

The project's innovation is concentrated on its facade system, which joins the building's solid wood structure on the southern side with an original projecting component of movable textile panels on which photovoltaic cells are arranged. These cells harness sunlight intelligently as they can move depending on the Sun's direction, producing energy while creating shaded areas in the summer.

The interiors use curtains, which are also mobile, to divide the spaces as the inhabitants like. In direct contact with the outer panels, these curtains use a LED system to supply additional light to the apartments.

S3/S31
Wilhelmsburg

13/34/151/152/154
156/252/640
Inselpark

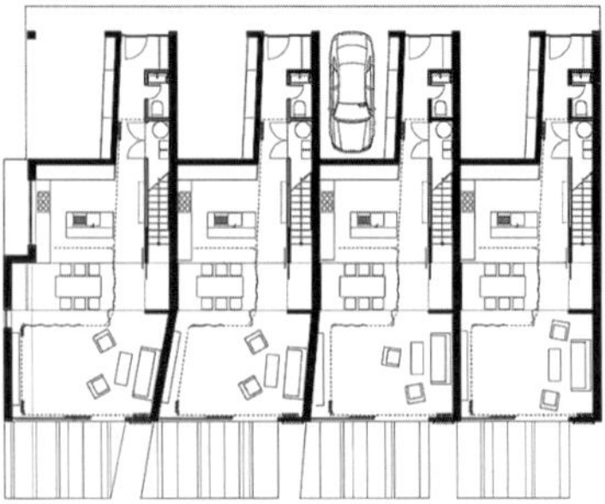

© IBA Hamburg / Kennedy & Violich Architecture

architects
Kennedy & Violich Architecture

type
residential

construction
2012-2013

78. Woodcube - Smart Material Houses

Am Inselpark 7
21109 Hamburg

external view only

www.iba-hamburg.de

S3/S31
Wilhelmsburg

13/34/151/152/154
156/252/640
Inselpark

Wood has been gaining increasing popularity in the construction industry. Awareness about the careful use of resources has ushered in major changes in the building sector. For instance, Woodcube's design shows how traditional techniques in solid wood constructions can be reconsidered through an impressive design.

Woodcube is a five-storey building made almost entirely of wood without glue or protective coverings. Wood is the defining material of the external facades as well as in the interiors, where all elements are wood. Wood forms the building's structure, and its 32-meter thick wood walls completely insulate the building.

The goal was to create a building that emits no greenhouse gases and is completely biodegradable. All materials used in the building were tested and non-renewable raw materials were avoided. Its electricity and heat are also from completely renewable energy sources.

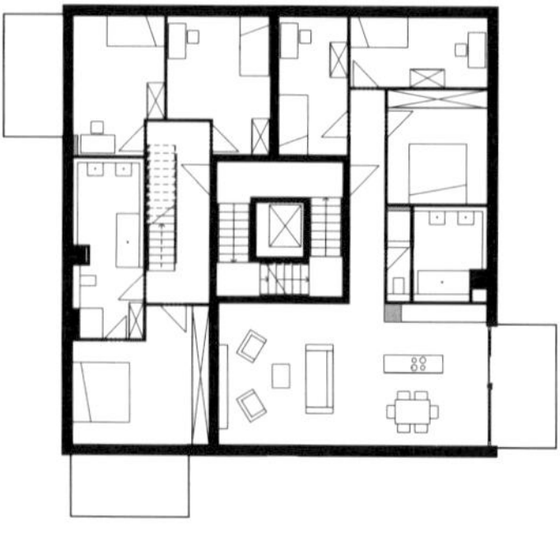

architects
IfuH, Architekturagentur

type
residential

construction
2012-2013

79. igs Center - Hybrid Houses

Neuenfelder Straße 9
21109 Hamburg

external view only

www.iba-hamburg.de

S3/S31
Wilhelmsburg

13/151/152/154/156 /252/640
Dratelnstraße
13/34/151/152/154 156/252/640
Inselpark

Excellent energy efficiency, contemporary design and versatile interiors were among the guiding lights of the igs Center design, the first completed Hybrid House.

The four-storey building is supported by reinforced concrete pillars, sunk into a small hill that contains the ground floor and exhibition areas. The upper floors rise of the hill and hold apartments and some offices. These functions can be switched at will because of the great versatility in the spaces' composition.

There are ten units inside the building. Each is in a U-shape arranged around a lobby that lets in light and can serve as a balcony. For the building's energy, a heat pump regulates the indoor temperature. In the winter, energy is extracted from the ground, and it is transferred back in the summer with a reverse process. The heat pump is turned off during the summer and the energy is sent to a cold storage system, which prevents the building from overheating, also aided by the green roof.

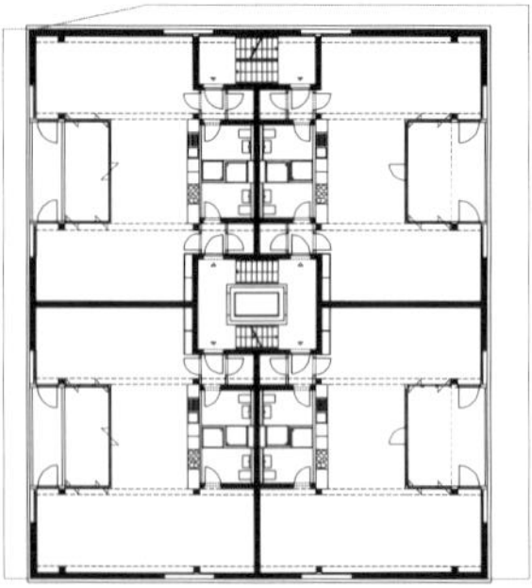

architects
Nägeliarchitekten

type
residential, hospitality, offices

construction
2010-2012

80. Ministry for Urban Development and the Environment

Neuenfelder Straße 19
21109 Hamburg

limited access

www.iba-hamburg.de

S3/S31
Wilhelmsburg

13/34/151/152/154
156/252/640
Inselpark

The building is like a colored ribbon that snakes through the center of Wilhelmsburg. It includes a 13-storey skyscraper and two five-storey wing buildings that follow the trajectory of a road and a railway line. To mediate in scale between the large complex and the user the wings are subdivided into seven separate "houses" linked along an internal street. Each "house" is grouped around an atrium with an open stairway for ease of orientation, providing huge reduction in energy use through natural cross ventilation and good interior lighting.

The pedestrian path is lined by public exhibition spaces, a conference area and a restaurant, all of which are visible through the large glass facade. The central atrium, at the base of the skyscraper, was designed like a large foyer, serving as a reception area for the offices and as a place to exhibit a large model of the city.

The coloured facade made of glazed ceramic panels is first of all providing the necessary attention that presents this important building as a beacon of change in the district. Secondly, its multiplicative colour scheme is deliberately trying to speak about pluralism and variety within one big organism, evoking the present and future culture of this district.

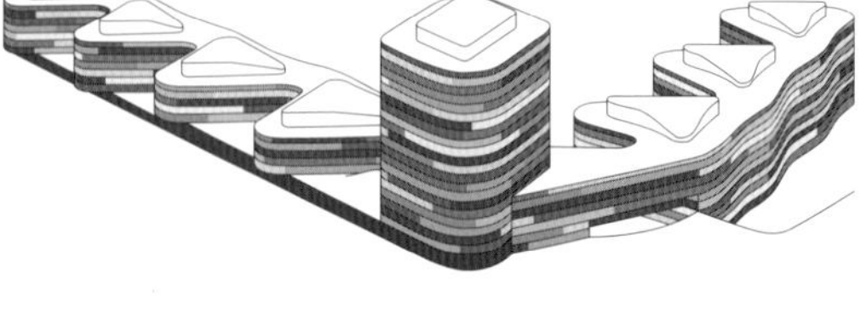

© Sauerbruch Hutton

architects
Sauerbruch Hutton

type
offices

construction
2011-2013

81. Tor zur Welt

Krieterstraße 5
21109 Hamburg

external view only

www.tor-zur-welt.hamburg.de

S3/S31
Wilhelmsburg

154
Thielenstraße

The school, whose name means "Gateway to the World", is an educational center with five central modules, including a school and business center, a environment and science center and a multipurpose building with a meeting room, cafe, and a training center for parents. In addition to the main modules, the center has a cafeteria for about 400 students, teachers, staff, and guests.

The multipurpose building is the core of the new educational center. Here the "gateway" opens outwards to welcome the entire city neighborhood to become a place for locals to gather and mingle. The "connection building" links all functions open to the public to the ground floor. It starts from the foyer of the multipurpose center and stretches along the "Street of Learning" towards hubs accessing to the school's different areas.

The complex was built with climatically sustainable materials and methods up to passive house standards, equipped with many solar panels. The main attraction is a "glass energy center" to let children experience environmental protection firsthand.

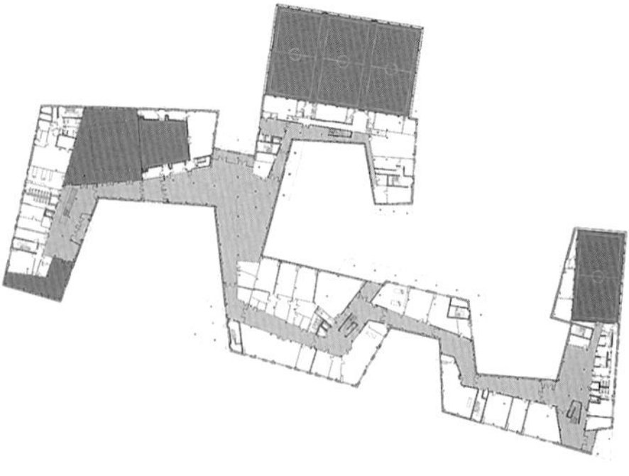

architects
bof architekten

type
school

construction
2011-2013

Museums

Africa Haus
Museum of Africa
-
Große Reichenstraße 27, 20457 Hamburg

www.afrika-haus.de
info@afrika-haus.de
Tel +49 (0)40 228605111

Bucerius Kunst Forum
Temporary art exhibitions
-
Alter Wall 12, 20457 Hamburg

www.buceriuskunstforum.de
info@buceriuskunstforum.de
Tel +49 (0)40 3609960

Deichtorhallen Hamburg
Contemporary art
-
Deichtorstraße 1, 20095 Hamburg

www.deichtorhallen.de
mail@deichtorhallen.de
Tel +49 (0)40 32103200

Designxport
Temporary design exhibitions
-
Hongkongstraße 8, 20457 Hamburg

designxport.de
mail@designxport.de
Tel +49 (0)40 303832650

Ernst Barlach Haus
Works by Ernst Barlach
and temporary exhibitions
-
Jenischpark Baron-Voght-Straße 50a-D,
22609 Hamburg

www.ernst-barlach-haus.de
info@barlach-haus.de
Tel +49 (0)40 828978
Fax +49 (0)40 826415

Hamburg Museum
History of the City of Hamburg
-
Holstenwall 24, 20355 Hamburg

shmh.de
info@mhg.shmh.de
Tel +49 (0)40 428132100

Hamburger Kunsthalle
Art from the Middle Ages to today
-
Glockengießerwall 5, 20095 Amburgo

www.hamburger-kunsthalle.de
info@hamburger-kunsthalle.de
Tel +49 (0)40 428131200

Internationales Maritimes Museum Hamburg
History and study of maritime
navigation
-
Kaispeicher B - Koreastraße 1
20457 Hamburg

www.immhh.de
info@imm-hamburg.de
Tel +49 (0)40 30092300
Fax +49 (0)40 300923045

Kesselhaus
Exhibition space dedicated
to HafenCity
-
Am Sandtorkai 30, 20457 Hamburg

www.hafencity.com/de/infocenter/das-hafencity-infocenter-im-kesselhaus.html
Tel +49 (0)40 36901799

Museum für Kunst und Gewerbe Hamburg
Museum of arts and crafts
-
Steintorplatz, 20099 Hamburg

www.mkg-hamburg.de
service@mkg-hamburg.de
Tel +49 (0)40 428134880
Fax +49 (0)40 428134999

Speicherstadtmuseum
History of the Speicherstadt (historical warehouse district)
-
Am Sandtorkai 36, 20457 Hamburg

www.speicherstadtmuseum.de
info@speicherstadtmuseum.de
Tel +49 (0)40 321191
Fax +49 (0)40 321530

Jenisch Haus
Museum of arts and culture
-
Baron-Voght-Straße 50, 22609 Hamburg

shmh.de/de/jenisch-haus
info@shmh.de
Tel +49 (0)40 76799654

Theaters

Allee Theater - Hamburger Kammeroper
-
Max-Brauer-Allee 76, 22765 Hamburg

www.hamburger-kammeroper.de
Tel +49 (0)40 382959

Das Schiff
-
Nikolaifleet, Holzbrücke 2, 20459 Hamburg

www.theaterschiff.de
Tel +49 (0)40 6965060

Deutsches Schauspielhaus
-
Kirchenallee 39, 20099 Hamburg

www.schauspielhaus.de
kontakt@schauspielhaus.de
Tel +49 (0)40 248713

Elbphilharmonie
-
Platz der Deutschen Einheit, 20457 Hamburg

www.elbphilharmonie.de
pavillon@elbphilharmonie.de
Tel +49 (0)40 35766666

Ernst Deutsch Theater
-
Friedrich-Schütter-Platz 1, 22087 Hamburg

www.ernst-deutsch-theater.de
info@ernst-deutsch-theater.de
Tel +49 (0)40 22701420
Fax: +49 (0)40 22701425

Staatsoper Hamburg
-
Große Theaterstraße 25, 20354 Hamburg

www.hamburgische-staatsoper.de
Tel +49 (0)40 356868

St. Pauli Theater
-
Spielbudenplatz 29-30, 20359 Hamburg

www.st-pauli-theater.de
Tel +49 (0)40 47110666

Restaurants

• • • expensive
• • mid-range
• inexpensive

Bullerei
• •
Lagerstraße 34b, 20357 Hamburg
bullerei.com
info@bullerei.com
Tel +49 (0)40 33442110

Café Leonar
•
Grindelhof 59, 20146 Hamburg
www.cafeleonar.de
cafe@cafeleonar.de
Tel +49 (0)40 41353011

CARLS an der Elbphilharmonie
• • •
Am Kaiserkai 69, 20457 Hamburg
www.carls-brasserie.de
carls@carls-brasserie.de
Tel +49 (0)40 300322400

Clouds
• •
Reeperbahn 1, 20359 Hamburg
clouds-hamburg.de
restaurant@clouds-hamburg.de
Tel +49 (0)40 30993280

Coast by East Hamburg
• •
Großer Grasbrook 14, 20457 Hamburg
www.coast-hamburg.de
info@coast-hamburg.de
Tel +49 (0)40 30993230

Restaurant Eisenstein
• • •
Friedensallee 9, 22765 Hamburg
restaurant-eisenstein.de
mail@restaurant-eisenstein.de
Tel +49 (0)40 3904606

Empire Riverside Restaurant
• • •
Bernhard-Nocht-Straße 97,
20359 Hamburg
www.restaurant-eisenstein.de
info@empire-riverside.de
Tel +49 (0)40 311190

Fillet of Soul
• •
Deichtorstraße 2, 20095 Hamburg
info@fillet-of-soul.de
Tel +49 (0)40 70705800

Fischereihafen Restaurant
• • •
Große Elbstraße 143, 22767 Hamburg
www.fischereihafenrestaurant.de
info@fischereihafenrestaurant.de
Tel +49 (0)40 381816
Fax +49 (0)40 3893021

Restaurant NIL
• •
Neuer Pferdemarkt 5, 20359 Hamburg
www.restaurant-nil.de
essen@restaurant-nil.de
Tel +49 (0)40 4397823

Santé
• •
Moorkamp 6, 20357 Hamburg
www.restaurant-sante.net
service@restaurant-sante.net
Tel +49 (0)40 228621300

Hotels

• • • expensive
• • mid-range
• inexpensive

25hours Hotel Hafencity
• • •
Überseeallee 5, 20457 Hamburg
www.25hours-hotels.com
hafencity@25hours-hotels.com
Tel +49 (0)40 2577770

Das kleine Schwarze
• •
Tornquiststraße 25, 20259 Hamburg
www.das-kleine-schwarze.com
hamburg@das-kleine-schwarze.com
Tel +49 (0)40 23939911

Empire Riverside Hotel
• • •
Bernhard-Nocht-Straße 97,
20359 Hamburg
www.empire-riverside.de
info@empire-riverside.de
Tel +49 (0)40 311190

Hadley's Bed and Breakfast
•
Beim Schlump 85, 20144 Hamburg
www.b-bhadleys.de
bed-breakfast@hamburg.de
Tel +49 (0)163 7956795

Henri Hotels
• • •
Bugenhagenstraße 21, 20095 Hamburg
www.henri-hotel.com
hello@henri-hotel.com
Tel +49 (0)40 5543570

My Place Hotel
• •
Lippmannstraße 5, 22769 Hamburg
www.myplace-hamburg.de
info@myplace-hamburg.de
Tel +49 (0)40 28571874

Raphael Hotel Wälderhaus
• •
Am Inselpark 19, 21109 Hamburg
www.raphaelhotelwaelderhaus.de
info@raphaelhotelwaelderhaus.de
Tel +49 (0)40 302156100
Fax +49 (0)40 302156103

Schlaflounge
•
Vereinsstraße 54b, 20357 Hamburg
www.schlaflounge.de
info@schlaflounge.de
Tel +49 (0)40 38688357
Fax +49 (0)40 38688358

Schlafschön
• •
Monetastraße 4, 20146 Hamburg
www.schlafschoen.com
barenscherhh@aol.com
Tel +49 (0)40 41354949
Fax +49 (0)40 41355050

SIDE Hotel
• • •
Drehbahn 49, 20354 Hamburg
www.side-hamburg.de
info@side-hamburg.de
Tel +49 (0)40 309990

Superbude St. Pauli
•
Juliusstraße 1-7, 22769 Hamburg
www.superbude.de
stpauli@superbude.com
Tel +49 (0)40 807915820

Architectual offices

Andreas Heller Architects & Designers
-
Am Sandtorkai 48, 20457 Hamburg

www.studio-andreas-heller.de
main@studio-andreas-heller.de
Tel +49 (0)40 4710380

baubüro.eins
-
Marschnerstieg 7, 22081 Hamburg

www.baubueroeins.de
info@baubueroeins.de
Tel +49 (0)40 210911690

Blauraum Architekten
-
Waterloohain 9, 22769 Hamburg

www.blauraum.eu
office@blauraum.eu
Tel +49 (0)40 419166910

bof architekten
-
Schillerstraße 47-49, 22767 Hamburg

www.bof-architekten.de
mail@bof-architekten.de
Tel +49 (0)40 38904380

Bruun & Möllers Landschaften
-
Ernst-Merck-Straße 12-14,
20099 Hamburg

www.bm-la.de
info@bm-la.de
Tel +49 (0)40 8227770

Carsten Roth Architekt
-
Waterloohain 5 A, 22769 Hamburg

www.carstenroth.com
Tel +49 (0)40 41125560

Christoph Konerding Architekt
-
Alsterdorfer Markt 6, 22297 Hamburg

konerding-architekt.de
buero@konerding-architekt.de
Tel +49 (0)40 4603064

gmp Architekten von Gerkan, Marg und Partner
-
Elbchaussee 139, 22763 Hamburg;
Rainvilleterrasse 4, 22765 Hamburg

www.gmp.de
info@gmp.de
Tel +49 (0)40 881510
Tel +49 (0)40 88151200

Hadi Teherani
-
Elbberg 1, 22767 Hamburg

www.haditeherani.com
architects@haditeherani.com
Tel +49 (0)40 248420

Hillmer und Richter Architekten GmbH
-
Reeperbahn 1, 20359 Hamburg

www.hillmerundrichter.de
info@hillmerundrichter.de
Tel +49 (0)40 22634990

Jens Bothe
-
Hohe Bleichen 13, 20354 Hamburg

www.jensbothe.de
mail@jensbothe.de
Tel +49 (0)40 4768680

KBNK Architekten
-
Große Rainstraße 39a, 22765 Hamburg

www.kbnk.de
office@kbnk.de
+49 (0)40 3992040

KPW Papay Warncke und Partner Architekten mbB
-
Michaelisstraße 22, D-20459 Hamburg

www.kpw-architekten.de
mail@kpw-architekten.de
Tel +49 (0)40 355550

MPP MEDING PLAN + PROJEKT GmbH
-
Auguststraße 14, D-22085 Hamburg

www.mpp.de
office@mpp.de
Tel +49 (0)40 4503070

Schenk Fleischhaker Architekten
-
Stahltwiete 19a, 22761 Hamburg

www.schenk-fleischhaker.de
architekten@schenk-fleischhaker.de
Tel +49 (0)40 398046780

SML Architekten
-
Schomburgstraße 120, 22767 Hamburg

www.sml-architekten.de
info@sml-architekten.de
Tel +49 (0)40 41364690

Spengler Wiescholek
-
Schomburgstraße 120, 22767 Hamburg

www.spengler-wiescholek.de
office@spengler-wiescholek.de
Tel +49 (0)40 3899860

Störmer Murphy and Partners
-
Michaelisbrücke 1, 20459 Hamburg

www.stoermer-partner.de
info@stoermer-partner.de
+49 (0)40 3697370

Winking · Froh Architekten
-
Brooktorkai 16, 20457 Hamburg

www.winking-froh.de
hamburg@winking-froh.de
Tel +49 (0)40 3749530

Index by architect

Index by project

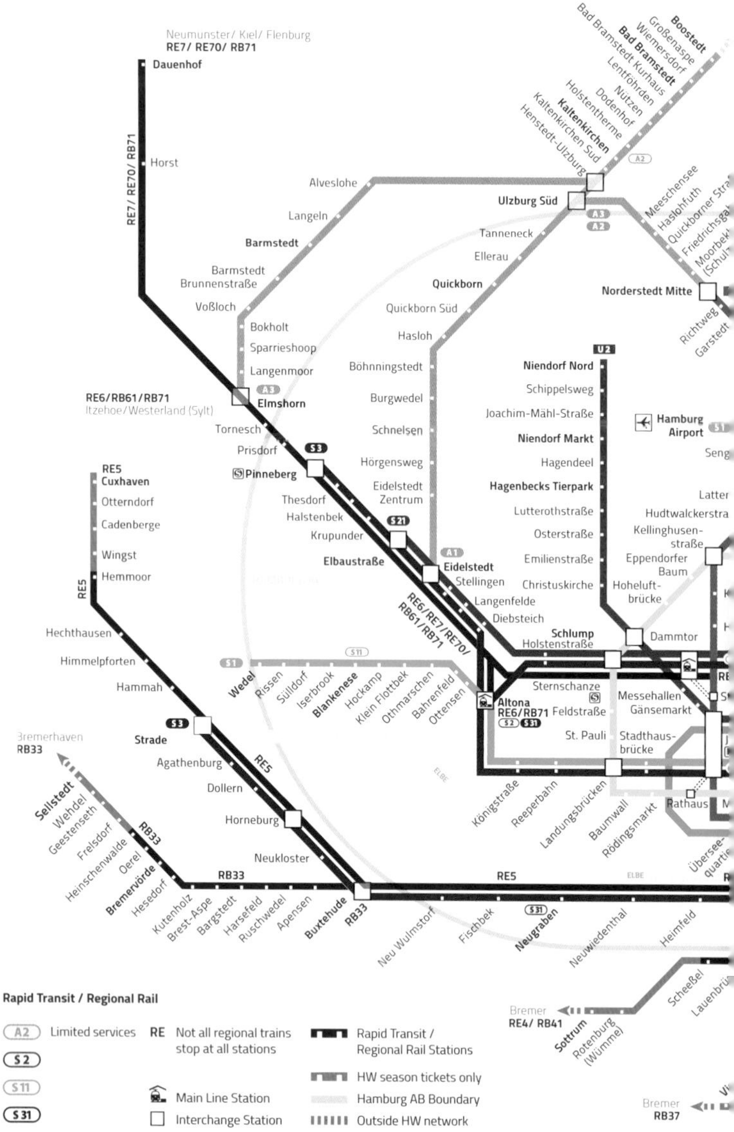

Neumunster/ Kiel/ Flenburg
RE7/ RE70/ RB71
Dauenhof
RE7/ RE70/ RB71
Horst
Alveslohe
Langeln
Barmstedt
Barmstedt Brunnenstraße
Voßloch
Bokholt
Sparrieshoop
Langenmoor
RE6/RB61/RB71
Itzehoe/Westerland (Sylt)
Elmshorn
A3
Tornesch
Prisdorf
S3
Pinneberg
Thesdorf
Halstenbek
Krupunder
S21
Elbaustraße
Boostedt
Großenaspe
Wiemersdorf
Bad Bramstedt
Bad Bramstedt Kurhaus
Lentföhrden
Nützen
Dodenhof
Holstentherme
Kaltenkirchen
Kaltenkirchen Süd
Henstedt-Ulzburg
A2
Ulzburg Süd
A3
A2
Tanneneck
Ellerau
Quickborn
Quickborn Süd
Hasloh
Böhnningstedt
Burgwedel
Schnelsen
Hörgensweg
Eidelstedt Zentrum
A1
Eidelstedt
Stellingen
Langenfelde
Diebsteich
RE6/RE7/RE70/RB61/RB71
Meeschensee
Haslohfuth
Quickborner Stra
Friedrichsga
Moorbek
Norderstedt Mitte
Richtweg
Garstedt
U2
Niendorf Nord
Schippelsweg
Joachim-Mähl-Straße
Niendorf Markt
Hagendeel
Hagenbecks Tierpark
Lutterothstraße
Osterstraße
Emilienstraße
Christuskirche
Hamburg Airport
S1
Seng
Latter
Hudtwalckerstra
Kellinghusenstraße
Eppendorfer Baum
Hoheluftbrücke
Schlump
Holstenstraße
Dammtor
Sternschanze
Messehallen
Gänsemarkt
Altona
RE6/RB71
S2
S31
Feldstraße
St. Pauli
Stadthausbrücke
Rathaus
S1
S11
Wedel
Rissen
Sülldorf
Iserbrook
Blankenese
Hockamp
Klein Flottbek
Othmarschen
Bahrenfeld
Ottensen
RE5
Cuxhaven
Otterndorf
Cadenberge
Wingst
Hemmoor
RE5
Hechthausen
Himmelpforten
Hammah
S3
Strade
Agathenburg
RE5
Dollern
Horneburg
Neukloster
ELBE
Königstraße
Reeperbahn
Landungsbrücken
Baumwall
Rödingsmarkt
Überseequartier
Bremerhaven
RB33
Sellstedt
Wehdel
Geestenseth
Frelsdorf
Heinschenwalde
Oerel
RB33
Bremervörde
Hesedorf
RB33
Kutenholz
Brest-Aspe
Bargstedt
Harsefeld
Ruschwedel
Apensen
Buxtehude
RB33
RE5
Neu Wulmstorf
Fischbek
S31
Neugraben
ELBE
Neuwiedenthal
Heimfeld
Scheeßel
Lauenbrü
Bremer
RE4/ RB41
Sottrum
Rotenburg (Wümme)
Bremer
RB37
Rapid Transit / Regional Rail
A2 Limited services
S2
S11
S31
RE Not all regional trains stop at all stations
Main Line Station
Interchange Station
Rapid Transit / Regional Rail Stations
HW season tickets only
Hamburg AB Boundary
Outside HW network

Neumünster
RB82
Rickling
Wahlstedt
Fahrenkrug
Bad Segeberg
RB82
Altengörs
Wakendorf
Fresenburg
Lübeck
RE8/RE80
Reinfeld (Holst)
Bad Oldesloe
RB81/RB82
Lübeck
RE83
Ratzeburg
Kupfermühle
Bargteheide
Gartenholz
Ahrensburg
Ahrensburg Ost
Schmalenbeck
Kiekut
Großhansdorf
U1
S1
S11
Ohlstedt
Hoisbüttel
Buckhorn
Volkdorf
Poppenbüttel
Wellingsbüttel
Hoheneichen
Kornweg
Meiendorfer Weg
Berne
Oldenfelde
Farmsen
Trabrennbahn
Buchenkamp
Ahrensburg West
RE8/RE80/RB81
Rahlstedt
Mölln (Lauenb)
Ohlsdorf
Rübenkamp
Alte Wöhr
Habichstraße
Saarland-
straße
U3
Wandsbek-
Gartenstadt
Alter
Teichweg
Straßburger
Straße
Wandsbeck
Markt
Tonndorf
Wandsbek
Barmbek
Dehnhaide
Hamburger Straße
Mundsburg
Uhlandstraße
Lübecker Straße
Lohhmühlenstraße
Friedrichs-
berg
Wandsbeker
Chausee
Ritterstraße
Wartenau
Landwehr
RE8/RE80/RB81
Hasselbrook
Berliner
Tor
Burgstraße
Hammer Kirche
Rauhes Hauss
Horner Rennbahn
Legienstraße
Billstedt
Merkenstraße
Steinfurther Allee
Mümmelmannsber
U2
U4
RE83
Nord
Haupt-
bahnhof
Central
Station
Süd
Rothenburgsort
Tiefstack
Billwerder-
Moorfleet
Mittlerer Landweg
Allermöhe
Nettelnburg
Bergedorf
Reinbek
Wohltorf
Aumühle
Schwarzenbek
Müssen
Hammerbrook
Elbbrücken
Veddel
Wilhelmsburg
RE3
RE4/RE5
RB31/RB41
RE1
Harburg
Meckelfeld
Hittfeld
Klecken
RE4/RB41
S2
RE1
S21
RE1
Büchen
Schwerin/ Rostock
RE1
Lauenburg (Elbe)
Echem
Maschen
Stelle
Ashausen
RE3/RB31
Winsen (Luhe)
Radbruch
Bardowick
Lüneburg
RE83/RB31/RB32
RE83
Wendisch Evern
Vastorf
Bavendorf
Dahlenburg
Neetzendorf
Göhrde
Leitsade
Hitzacker
Dannenberg
Ost
RB32
RE3/RB31
RB32
Suerhop
Holm-Seppensen
Büsenbachtal
Handeloh
Wintermoor
Schneverdinger
Wolterdingen
Soltau Nord
RB38
RE3
Bienenbüttel
Bad Bevensen
Uelzen
RE2/RE20
RB37/RB47
Wieren
Soltendieck
Schnega
RE20/RB47
Magdeburg
RE20
Munster (Örtze)
Brockhöfe
Ebstorf (Uelzen)
RE2/RE3
Suderburg
Stederdorf
(Kr. Uelzen)
Bad
Bodenteich
Hannover
RB38
RB37
Hannover/ Gottingen
RE2/RE3
Braunschweig
RB47

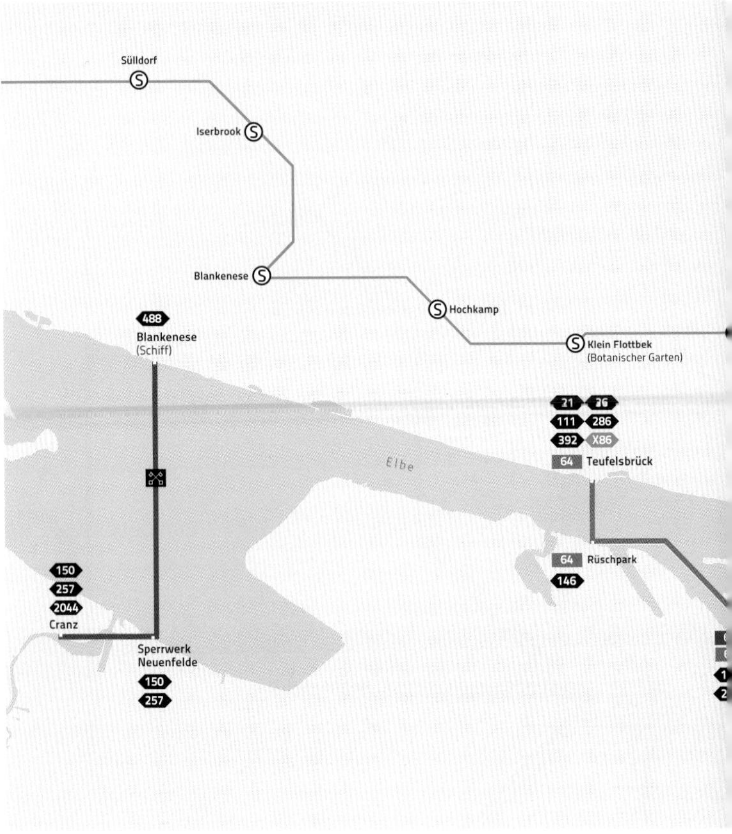

Harbour Ferries

HADAG Ferry

61 HVV Ferry

62

72

73

75

Rapid Transit (connecting)

21 111 X86 Buses (connecting)

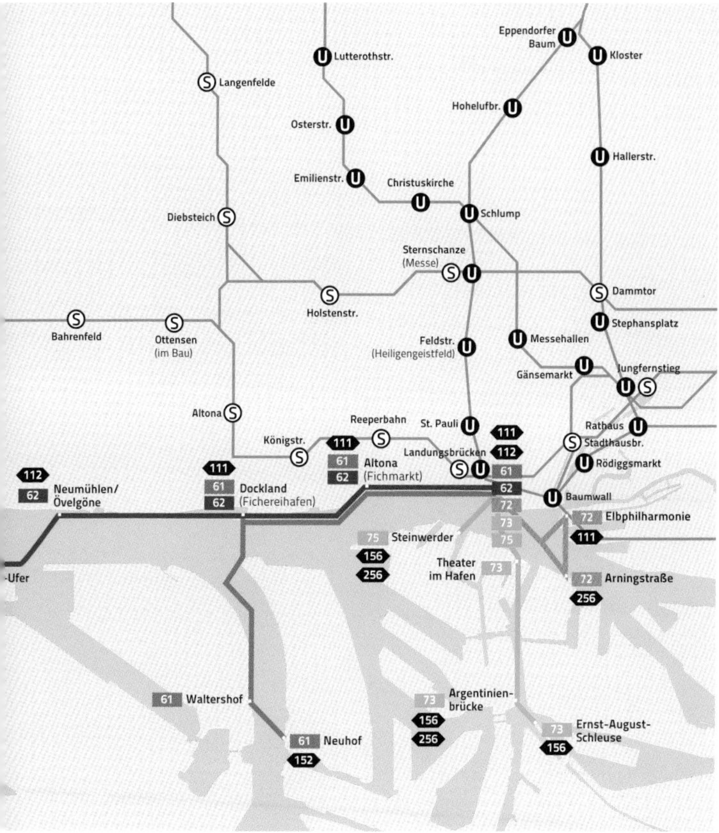

Eppendorfer Baum
Kloster
Lutterothstr.
Langenfelde
Hoheluftbr.
Osterstr.
Hallerstr.
Emilienstr.
Christuskirche
Schlump
Diebsteich
Sternschanze (Messe)
Dammtor
Holstenstr.
Stephansplatz
Bahrenfeld
Ottensen (im Bau)
Feldstr. (Heiligengeistfeld)
Messehallen
Gänsemarkt
Jungfernstieg
Altona
Reeperbahn
St. Pauli
Rathaus
Königstr.
Stadthausbr.
Landungsbrücken
Rödiggsmarkt
112
62 Neumühlen/ Övelgöne
111
61 Dockland
62 (Fichereihafen)
111
61 Altona
62 (Fichmarkt)
111
112
61
62
72
73
75
Baumwall
72 Elbphilharmonie
111
75 Steinwerder
156
256
Theater im Hafen 73
72 Arningstraße
256
-Ufer
61 Waltershof
61 Neuhof
152
73 Argentinien-brücke
156
256
73 Ernst-August-Schleuse
156

Photolithography
LAB di Gallotti Giuseppe Fulvio, Florence

This volume was printed in August 2020
by Gutenberg Press Limited, Gudja Road,
Tarxien, Malta PLA 19